An End to Welfare Rights:
The Rediscovery of Independence

The IEA Health and Welfare Unit

Choice in Welfare No. 49

An End to Welfare Rights:
The Rediscovery of Independence

David G. Green

IEA Health and Welfare Unit
London

First published March 1999

The IEA Health and Welfare Unit
2 Lord North St
London SW1P 3LB

ISBN 0-255 36452-0
ISSN 1362-9565

Typeset by the IEA Health and Welfare Unit
in Century Schoolbook 10.5 point
Printed in Great Britain by
St Edmundsbury Press Ltd
Bury St Edmunds, Suffolk

Contents

The Author

David G. Green is the Director of the Health and Welfare Unit at the Institute of Economic Affairs. His books include *Power and Party in an English City*, Allen & Unwin, 1980; *Mutual Aid or Welfare State*, Allen & Unwin, 1984 (with L. Cromwell); *Working-Class Patients and the Medical Establishment*, Temple Smith/ Gower, 1985; *The New Right: The Counter Revolution in Political, Economic and Social Thought*, Wheatsheaf, 1987; *Reinventing Civil Society*, IEA, 1993; *Community Without Politics*, IEA, 1996; and *Benefit Dependency*, IEA, 1998.

He wrote the chapter on 'The Neo-Liberal Perspective' in *The Student's Companion to Social Policy*, Blackwell, 1998.

Acknowledgements

I am very grateful to two anonymous referees for some very useful comments and to Lord Harris of High Cross for intellectual inspiration over the years. I am also indebted to Alan Deacon and Lawrence Mead for occasional, but invaluable, discussions over the last year or two. Particular thanks go to my colleague at the IEA, Robert Whelan.

David G. Green

Acknowledgements

Introduction

During the heyday of political paternalism in the 1960s and 1970s, it became common to speak of the 'rediscovery of poverty'. Today, New Labour's explicit denunciation of Old Labour's enthusiasm for solving problems with 'more money' signifies the beginning of a new emphasis in social policy—the 'rediscovery of independence'. The phrase 'work for those who can; security for those who cannot' has come to encapsulate the efforts of the Blair Government to reform welfare, and policies announced so far suggest a stronger focus on the reciprocal obligations of the individual rather than 'welfare rights'. However, most of the policies imposed during the age of paternalism remain intact and the measures so far advocated by the Government only scratch at the surface. Closer examination suggests that, while New Labour has shed many of the simplistic prescriptions of Old Labour, especially its egalitarianism, it has retained much of its paternalism.

Welfare reform should be based on high expectations of human potential. In a free society, individuals can be expected to make provision for the normal expenses of living, periods during the lifecycle when expenditure will be high (child-raising) or income low (retirement), and to provide against possible misfortunes. Moreover, individuals can reasonably be expected to choose a family structure that will allow them to support and care for children, if they have any.

The Government's strategy of 'making work pay', however, is not only too narrow, it is also very unlikely to achieve its declared aim of reducing benefit dependency. Its continuing paternalism has led the Government to encourage claimants to take a job by paying them additional in-work benefits. This subsidisation reduces the number of people *wholly* reliant on benefits by increasing the number *partially* reliant on welfare. Consequently, it is creating a new kind of in-work dependency and I will advocate instead measures that encourage self-sufficiency. In addition, the Government's policies will continue to encourage family breakdown which, in turn, will further increase reliance on benefits.

Two main proposals are made. First, that we urgently need to redefine the social contract between the community and its members. The safety net should always be there to prevent hardship, but we need to reconsider what the members of a society can reasonably expect of benefit claimants. This publication suggests a different method of combining an ever-present safety net with a stronger focus on self-sufficiency.

Second, we should abolish all entitlements to benefit and, instead, place a two-part obligation on the Government: to provide assistance sufficient to prevent severe hardship for all who ask; and to do so in a manner most likely to lead to self-sufficiency.

The study is organised as follows. Chapter 1 describes the current Government's policies, and questions their factual basis. Chapter 2 provides an historical perspective on today's policy debate by providing an overview of public policy from Tudor times until Beveridge. Chapter 3 describes the rise of the egocentric welfare ethos that emerged during the post-war years and how it came under effective challenge from the 1980s onwards. Chapter 4 considers how best to replace public policies that currently encourage welfare dependency with alternatives based, as far as possible, on self-sufficient families.

Summary

Chapter 1

Four main influences underlie the Blair Government's proposals:

- Rejection of the 'rights culture' in favour of the belief that individuals should work if they are able.

- The assumption that worklessness is the result of barriers.

- Rejection of the old egalitarianism, but a continuing interest in redistribution to the 'deserving poor'.

- Ambiguity about the family, which reflects a conflict between two groups: those who favour anti-family social engineering to bring about the equalisation of gender roles; and those who see the 'family based on marriage' as the main social building block.

The Government's argument that worklessness is the result of barriers is challenged. Four main barriers have been identified: childcare costs, stigma, the unemployment trap and the poverty trap.

Childcare costs are shown to be not as significant as the Government claims and stigma to be of little or no relevance. The unemployment trap is not a barrier in the ordinary sense. A person who refrains from work because it does not pay is making a financial judgement, not facing an obstacle. Similarly the poverty trap is not a barrier. Moreover, its impact is much smaller than the Government claims.

The Government's flagship reform, the working families tax credit, is a rebadged family credit with the same faults. Family credit has displaced work effort by wives in couples and by custodial lone parents. And it has encouraged family breakdown. The working families tax credit will have the same effects, and in addition will encourage in-work benefit dependency, not least by replacing total reliance on income support with partial reliance on benefits.

3

The cost of family breakdown to the social security budget already exceeds the cost of unemployment. In 1997/98 the total cost of benefits for lone parents in Great Britain was £10 billion and of unemployment, £6.1 billion. Normally, when unemployment is low, social security spending falls, but in recent years this tendency has been counterbalanced by the rising cost of family breakdown.

Chapter 2

Since Tudor times policy makers have grappled with the problem that having a safety net, of itself, tends to reduce work effort. Earlier reforms are described, especially the 1834 new poor law which was based on a 'self-acting' test—that is, help was provided on workhouse terms to all who asked, without a means test. However, life in the workhouse was intended to be less attractive than that of the independent labourer.

The ethos had changed by the end of the nineteenth century. Typical of thinkers at the turn of the century was Helen Bosanquet, who urged a 'positive' rather than a deterrent approach. Many different types of people needed help, she said, and the underlying causes of their immediate problem should be discovered and help given to restore independence wherever possible. The issue was not help or neglect, but how best to provide restorative help.

During the twentieth century commitment to personal responsibility has weakened gradually. By focusing on the 'poverty line', studies by Booth and Rowntree, for example, directed attention towards the symptom of an underlying problem. However, by the time of the Beveridge report, the sense of mutual obligation and the commitment to family self-sufficiency, though weakened, remained intact.

Chapter 3

Theories of social exclusion and victim status, following what many have called the 'rediscovery' of poverty in the 1960s, led to the abandonment of personal responsibility as a guiding principle of welfare reform. By the 1970s public policies were influenced by a doctrine that can be called 'egocentric collectivism'. It embraced four main ideas:

- *Social determinism*. Individuals were seen as powerless and 'the system' dominant, from which it was concluded that holding individuals responsible was 'blaming the victim' and the only effective action was, not social amelioration, but mass political action.

- *Egalitarianism*. The powers of the state should be used forcibly to bring about equal income and wealth or at least to compress differentials.

- *Welfare rights*. Individuals have one-sided claims on the public purse, with little or no acknowledgement of corresponding obligations.

- *Cultural nihilism*. Individuals should be released from moral and cultural restraints.

The high point of this doctrine came during the 1970s, and over the next decade a counter-movement developed which might be called the 'rediscovery of independence'. Led by writers such as Charles Murray and Lawrence Mead, it rejected the egocentric rights culture and asserted the importance of a two-sided ideal of community and self-sufficiency. The community should always maintain a safety net and individuals should work, if at all possible.

Three main approaches to reform emerged from this counter attack: the restoration of functions to civil society; reciprocal obligation; and making work pay.

Chapter 4

We should reform social security based on the assumption that there is a contract between the individual and society. All entitlements to benefit should be abolished and a twofold obligation placed on the Government: to provide assistance sufficient to prevent severe hardship to all who ask; and to do so in a manner most likely to lead to self-sufficiency. To that end, the chief means-tested income replacement benefits should be cancelled and transitional assistance introduced in their stead. National insurance should be abolished to end the pretence that benefits have been earned.

Work should be a requirement of the benefit system. Reasonable work obligations for three groups are suggested: the able bodied, lone parents, and disabled people unable to be wholly self-sufficient through work.

For the able bodied, full-time work is a reasonable expectation.

Where there are two living parents, one-parent families should be self-sufficient. Absent lone parents should be expected to pay sufficient maintenance to keep their children, and custodial lone parents should be required to work as many hours as necessary to keep themselves off benefits.

Disabled people should try to be as self-sufficient as their disability allows.

New applicants for benefit should be subject to strict requirements before any benefit is paid. All new applicants should meet a personal adviser to determine their capacity for self-sufficiency. It is reasonable to expect people to have sufficient savings to cover two weeks without income and so anyone wanting cash assistance should be required to take part in two weeks of job search before benefit is payable. Any emergency cash assistance required during that time should be treated as a repayable loan.

A graded series of alternatives should also be provided for people not yet ready for full-time work. But unsubsidised work should always be the first choice, with other options only temporary until the ultimate objective of unsubsidised paid employment is met. Training should not be ranked as an equal alternative to work.

If a person works full time and is still unable to command a 'living wage', an in-work benefit may be defensible. Family credit and working families tax credit have damaging side-effects. They require only 16 hours work a week, with the result that many reduce their work effort to qualify. This defect could be avoided by defining full-time work as 40 hours a week for 50 weeks a year (or 50 hours a week when the children reach school age). Parents with dependent children, whose income was still very low after putting in that amount of effort, would be considered by most people as deserving of assistance.

In addition to provision for a 40/50-hour supplement, the working families tax credit should be abolished and tax allowances reformed to encourage marriage. Married couples should each have a transferable tax allowance in addition to the married person's allowance. Child benefit should be abolished and replaced by child tax allowances.

Tax allowances permit people to keep their own money and thereby encourage a sense of personal responsibility. Benefits tend to have the opposite effect. The chief argument against tax allowances is that people who have no tax liability (because their income is below the tax threshold) do not benefit. The counter argument is that the existence of the allowance gives people an incentive to earn more so that they are able to take advantage of the whole tax allowance.

The state retirement age should be phased out by raising it in stages of six months per year, so that in 10 years it will be 70 and, in 20 years, 75. Individuals who have not saved enough to give up work should be expected to carry on working until illness or frailty intervenes, when the equivalent of the current incapacity benefit should be available.

The basic state pension and SERPS (or any subsequent mandatory state second pension) should be abolished, but not for existing recipients. Obligations under SERPS should be met.

As far as possible, a tax regime that is neutral towards all forms of saving should be implemented.

Once the state's role has been confined to maintaining a safety net and a light regulatory regime, individuals would be free to pursue strategies for self-sufficiency. The most obvious would be a cross-generational strategy backed up by an ethos of 'work till you drop'.

The end result would be a maximum of self-sufficiency with an infallible safety net for anyone who falls on hard times for whatever reason.

1

New Labour's Strategy for the Workless

SOON after coming into office in May 1997 the Blair Government announced its 'new deal' for the workless, accompanied by a heightened emphasis on the duties as well as the rights of citizenship. The new deal for the 18-24 age group originally offered four options for those who had been receiving jobseeker's allowance (JSA) for six months: subsidised work, full-time training or education, work for a voluntary organisation, or work for the environmental taskforce. There was no 'fifth option' of remaining on benefit.[1] Subsequently self-employment has been added. However, under the new deals for the long-term unemployed, lone parents, the disabled and partners of the unemployed there is no obligation to work or train. Proposals for a 'single gateway' to benefit will mean that from April 2000 it will be a condition of benefit that individuals must attend an interview 'to talk about their prospects of finding work'.[2] Moreover, the publication of the welfare green paper and the announcement of the working families tax credit during the March 1998 Budget statement suggested a shift in emphasis from the obligations of citizenship to 'making work pay'.

The Government's green paper on welfare reform identifies 'three key problems'. One of them is that: 'people face a series of barriers to paid work, including financial disincentives'.[3] In other words, the Government makes the assumption that the great majority of the workless want to work but are prevented from doing so by barriers. It concludes that public policy should remove these obstacles. Four main barriers have been identified.

1. *The cost of childcare*
According to the 1998 *Financial Statement and Budget Report* (FSBR), the Government is determined to 'ensure that no parent

8

should be unable to take up the opportunity to work through a lack of access to affordable quality childcare'.[4]

2. *Stigma*

The Government believes that the stigma attached to welfare benefits discourages take-up and, consequently, family credit is to be replaced by a tax credit. According to a Government discussion paper: 'As a tax credit rather than a welfare benefit, it will reduce the stigma associated with claiming in-work support, and encourage higher take-up. Its clear link with employment should demonstrate the rewards of work over welfare and help ensure that people move off welfare into work'.[5]

3. *Work does not pay: the unemployment trap*

Discussions of incentives usually distinguish between the unemployment trap and the poverty trap. The unemployment trap describes the situation of a person who is not working at all and would not be financially better off in work, or would not be very much better off. The usual measure of the strength of the unemployment trap is the replacement ratio. Income on benefit is expressed as a percentage of a person's previous wage or the likely future wage an individual could earn. A person with a 100 per cent replacement ratio has no financial incentive to work and the Government has reduced the percentage by increasing in-work benefits. In the 1998 FSBR Gordon Brown stated that, 'People are understandably reluctant to take work that does not pay'. Therefore, work and opportunity are to be 'encouraged and rewarded, rather than penalised'.[6] According to the Chancellor, the 1998 Budget reduced the unemployment trap by ensuring that a couple earning £200 with two young children would be £23 a week better off in work than on benefit.

4. *Work does not pay: the poverty trap*

The poverty trap refers to people already in work but receiving in-work benefits and paying taxes. The combination of taxes and benefit withdrawal can mean that an individual (or household) does not benefit financially from increased hours of work. The usual technical term for the loss per pound of extra income is the marginal deduction rate (or effective marginal tax rate). In some cases the rate can exceed 100 per cent. A person faced with a high

marginal deduction rate is usually less willing to add to his hours
of work. Thus, a part-time worker may be less likely to move to
full-time work, or he may decline overtime, or refrain from taking
a second job or casual work. If the income test is a household test,
other family members may refrain from work. The Government
believes its measures will also 'ease' the poverty trap by reducing
the taper under family credit (to be renamed working families tax
credit) from 70 per cent to 55 per cent.

The Government's focus on the removal of barriers assumes that
people are on welfare rather than in work because something
beyond their control has prevented them from taking a job. It
assumes that they are not responsible for their circumstances and
that they are powerless to change their situation unless someone
else (the Government) alters it. The counter view makes two main
assumptions. First, that people are often responsible for their
circumstances, at least to some extent. And second, that on those
occasions when individuals find themselves in circumstances
neither of their own choosing, nor their own making, then public
policies should not encourage passivity, but rather aim to stimu-
late active efforts to overcome obstacles.

Despite some of its rhetoric, the Government is reluctant to hold
individuals responsible and the result has been an emphasis on
explanations that diminish personal responsibility. Most notably
it has defined a 'financial disincentive' as a 'barrier'. In reality,
however, responding to an incentive is a decision. Some individuals decide not to work because they can get as much as they want
on benefit. No outside obstacle prevents them from working. As I
will show below, other people in the same predicament have
chosen to work despite both the poverty trap and the unemployment trap.

Before going any further, it will be useful to examine whether or
not the factual assumptions behind the working families tax credit
are justified. A very useful body of evidence has been put together
during the 1990s by the Department of Social Security (DSS) in
conjunction with the Policy Studies Institute (PSI). The DSS/PSI
Programme of Research into Low-Income Families (PRILIF) began
in 1991 with a sample of 2,200 low-income families. In 1993 a
further sample of 1,000 families leaving family credit was studied.
Sub-sets were followed up in 1993, 1994, 1995 and 1996.[7]

Childcare

First, to what extent is childcare a barrier to work? Reuben Ford conducted a DSS/PSI study of 850 lone parents in and out of work in 1994, with 60 follow-ups in 1995. The study found that the most common forms of childcare were unpaid, including help from partners, relatives, working only school hours, or leaving the children to fend for themselves. About 70 per cent of lone parents in work were not paying for childcare and of the 30 per cent of working lone parents who *were* paying, the average payment was £33.20 a week in 1994, though half paid less than £25.00.[8] Working lone parents who paid for childcare paid an average of £1.01 for each hour of work (50 per cent paid less than 88p), accounting for one-fifth of their after-tax earnings.[9]

Ford asked out-of-work lone parents what arrangements they would make if they worked. One in six (17 per cent) said their parents would care for the children (actual use of parents by lone parents in work was 29 per cent).[10] A further one in six said they would use other relatives or friends.[11] Only half expected to use paid or unpaid childcare at all. About 25 per cent said they would only work during school hours. (This was true of 15 per cent of working lone parents.)[12]

The study concluded that childcare was 'some part of the problem' of work entry for more than half the respondents out of work.[13] But overall, lone parents made a calculation in which childcare played only a part.[14] They considered the gains from work, including the net wage (allowing for costs), the social benefits of working (getting out of the house or making new friends), in-work benefits, and the potential child-development advantages of childcare. The gains from not working included the high out-of-work income, traditions of 'good mothering', avoiding the hassle of juggling childcare and work, and fears about the quality of childcare.[15] The most common reason for not working was that the children were too young, given in 40 per cent of cases.[16] About a quarter of respondents calculated that they were financially better off not working.[17]

The key finding, according to Ford, was: 'that childcare was not the major barrier for the majority of lone mothers'. They had 'other problems that needed to be resolved as well'. In all, just one

in 12 out-of-work lone parents said that childcare difficulties alone
kept them out of work.[18] Summing up Ford's findings, Alan Marsh,
who has headed the DSS/PSI studies, concluded that childcare is
a problem for lone parents but 'in many ways, it is the least of
their problems'.[19]

These findings are consistent with US experience. US workfare
programmes have typically made childcare readily available, but
it has often not been taken up. The Massachusetts Employment
and Training Choices Program funded childcare for workfare more
generously than any other state and found that only 14 per cent
of participants asked for care from the programme. In San Diego,
California, where strenuous efforts were made to secure 100 per
cent participation in workfare, only 12 per cent claimed reim-
bursement for childcare costs.[20]

In the light of this evidence, it is not obvious why the Government's policy puts such confidence in payment of childcare costs
as a method of encouraging more lone mothers to work. This
policy appears to be driven by another imperative: anti-family
social engineering, to which I will return later.

Stigma and Take-Up

How important is 'stigma' in deterring eligible individuals from
claiming family credit? A 1991 survey had found 64 per cent take-
up among those thought to be eligible and, on behalf of the DSS,
McKay and Marsh then went back to eligible non-claimants in
1993 to find out why they had not claimed. They interviewed 72
couples who were thought to be still eligible for family credit in
1993 and carried out in-depth interviews with a further 40
couples. The results of the 72 interviews found that 21 per cent
could not be classified, 17 per cent were on family credit, 12 per
cent were eligible but not receiving benefit, 28 per cent were *not*
eligible because their earnings were too high, and 22 per cent were
out of work (and therefore not eligible).[21] They concluded that a
proportion of the 1991 sample had not been eligible after all, so
that the take-up rate of 64 per cent should 'almost certainly' have
been higher.[22]

The in-depth interviews tried to understand the impact of stigma
and found that the issue was 'commonly mentioned'. It was

'something that entered their minds, even though they may have considered it and then given it little credence'. One claimant had said: 'Some people have their pride, but that's all gone out of the window really now, hasn't it?'[23]

Marsh and McKay concluded that stigma was of little practical importance:

> Little evidence was found that eligible non-claimants feared stigma or criticism. Indeed questioning on this point showed that almost everyone who applied had found their friends and relatives either neutral or supportive... A series of questions on the desirability of benefits drew no sign either that there was any widespread stigma attached to claiming, or that this was something peculiar to eligible non-claimants.[24]

By 1997 Marsh had concluded that 'the more you learn about eligible non-claimants, the less eligible they become'.[25] Moreover, he believed that the true take-up rates of 70-80 per cent represented a practical maximum.[26]

Transforming family credit from a welfare benefit into a tax credit in the hope of reducing stigma appears, therefore, unlikely to increase take-up.

The Poverty Trap and the Unemployment Trap

The Government claims that the high marginal deduction rates faced by family credit claimants discourage them from working longer hours. As a result the benefit withdrawal rate has been reduced from 70 per cent to 55 per cent.

However, evidence from the Department of Social Security's PRILIF series of studies suggests that the poverty trap made little difference to the decision to work. According to Marsh, 'The evidence was that if the withdrawal rate was increased to, say, 100 per cent, few would notice and no-one would behave any differently'. It would normally be assumed that a high marginal deduction rate would reduce the incentive to work additional hours, just as higher tax rates are assumed to make a difference, at the margin, to the willingness to work. However, under family credit the effect of the withdrawal rate is cushioned by the six-month award period. Family credit is assessed over approximately four to six weeks and awarded for six months regardless of any changes in circumstance. Thus, an individual offered overtime during the six months can earn the additional income, and is under no obligation to notify the DSS. Such income is, of course, taxable but does not affect family credit payments. (The six-month payment period continues under working families tax credit.) Alan Marsh concluded that:

> In most claimants' and ex-claimants' views, more earnings are more earnings and will be welcomed... Improved labour market positions are rarely to be rejected solely on the ground of loss of benefit... The poverty trap may be an inequity but it is rarely experienced that way. It is the unemployment trap that counts.[27]

Moreover, evidence from a variety of studies (the 1991 survey and follow-ups of lone parents in 1992, 1993, 1994, 1995 and 1996) led Marsh to believe that 'about half the people who work in jobs whose basic wage would qualify them for in-work benefits, work overtime instead, or they live with a second earner or, more rarely, they do a second job'.[28] Marsh believed this was because:

> social conventions, roles and expectations, as well as individual ambitions, are stronger determinants of work than marginal changes in the ratio between wages and benefits'.[29]

However, Marsh argues that family credit did help to spring the unemployment trap by widening the gap between income in work compared with benefit while out of work. Families on family credit had higher incomes than if they had been on income support. In 1991 lone parents had been £30 a week better off and couples £18. In 1994, lone parents were £44 better off. The 1994 survey suggested that lone parents on family credit working as few as 16-23 hours, if they were receiving maintenance, were nearly 60 per cent better off in work. They would have received £94 on income support compared with £146 on family credit.[30]

As a result, family credit was responsible for a significant movement of people from income support to work. Based on the PRILIF, some 54 per cent of lone parents and 36 per cent of couples on family credit had prior experience of income support before claiming family credit. All told, nearly half had moved directly from income support into work plus family credit.[31]

Another study for the DSS found that one-third of parents who left income support had done so expecting to receive family credit. From their survey responses, the investigators thought that about half of them might not have left income support without family credit.[32]

Thus, the evidence from a long series of studies is that the 70 per cent family-credit taper has not made a substantial difference to the willingness to work. The payment of benefits to create a substantial gap between total in-work income and out-of-work benefit, however, has encouraged many benefit recipients, especially lone mothers, to work.

Policies calculated to increase the gap between in-work income and out-of-work benefit are, therefore, likely from this experience to encourage more people to work, but a minor adjustment of the marginal deduction rate (from 70 per cent to 55 per cent) is unlikely to make a major impact. Moreover, the change in the taper means that, without any behavioural change, more people will automatically be eligible for the working families tax credit, a further problem to which I return below.

So far I have argued that, contrary to the assumptions of the Government, the evidence shows that childcare costs, stigma, the poverty trap and the unemployment trap are not insurmountable 'barriers'. Each is best understood as one of several factors affecting human motivation. Theories which rest on financial incentives or assume the presence of insurmountable barriers are incomplete. Other influences are at work, with the result that public policy measures often produce unanticipated behavioural effects. Family credit has been no exception.

Behavioural Effects of In-Work Benefits

Analysis of family credit reveals that it has had some unwanted side-effects. In particular, there is evidence that family credit has displaced work effort.

First, how many people are affected? In February 1998 there were 760,000 family credit claimants in Great Britain. Of these, 658,000 were employees and 103,000 were self-employed. 391,000 were couples and 370,000 (49 per cent) lone parents, all but 15,000 female.[33] That is, two main groups claim family credit: lone parents and single earners in a couple.

Marsh and McKay compared the extent to which wives in couples worked by comparing three groups: family credit claimants, eligible non-claimants and those on 'moderate income' (defined as between one per cent and 25 per cent above the maximum for receipt of family credit for the family size).[34] They found that six per cent of family credit wives in couples worked, compared with 10 per cent of wives among eligible non-claimants and 31 per cent of those in couples on 'moderate income'.[35] In the latter case, it was because the wife worked that the couple were in the 'moderate-income' group.[36]

It may be that the wives who wished to work did so regardless of the benefit system and that wives who put caring for their young children above work would have refrained from work, whatever the benefit system. The evidence of the PRILIF suggests only that benefits are *among* the influences shaping the preferences of many people. Family credit has made it possible for single earners in couples to top up their income so that their partners can remain at home caring for the children. Such couples could have avoided claiming if the wife had worked part time, or if they had saved enough before the children came along to allow the wife to stay off work to perform the vital task of child raising. Family credit allows them to rely on benefits instead.

It is difficult to disentangle the behavioural effects of benefits from the personal preferences that guide people in judging whether to go out to work or care for their children. But regardless of their relative importance, the present Government assumes that 'making work pay' through working families tax credit will reduce benefit dependency and, by implication, increase self-sufficiency. Experience of family credit, however, is that for couples it is associated with reduced willingness to work and diminished self-sufficiency. It may be admirable for a mother to care for her own children, but it would be even more admirable if she did so without relying on benefits.

Family credit has had a different effect on lone parents. In their case it appears to reduce incentives for improving skills and earnings. Alex Bryson and colleagues found that lone mothers on family credit were likely to be earning less than others not on family credit but with similar educational qualifications.

Using the PRILIF sample, they compared lone parents on family credit with those in work but not claiming in two years: 1991 and 1995. By 1995, the family credit recipients were earning 37 per cent less per week than non-recipients, allowing for 'their human capital and other characteristics'.[37] This difference was partly due to the number of hours worked, but a significant difference of 28 per cent remained for hourly earnings. They concluded that family credit may discourage lone mothers from improving their skills or seeking promotion. As Jane Millar and her colleagues concluded from the same evidence, family credit gives a 'significant boost to income in work but this may be at the cost of preventing people from improving their long-term earnings capacity'.[38]

Marsh and McKay concluded that family credit improved incentives to get a paid job in the first place but at the expense of reducing the incentives of those with jobs to work more hours or take a better-paid job. In their own words, 'while family credit clearly offers help with the first step—getting a job at all—it may act as a hindrance to further steps—improving earnings by overtime, promotion, or a second earner'.[39]

According to Marsh, the consequence was that 'in-work benefits may re-create in work the poverty and dependence they are supposed to abolish out of work'.[40] This tendency mainly affects lone parents. Among couples the vast majority of family-credit claimants were male earners: 300,000 out of the 391,000.[41] Usually they were sole earners with young children and a wife not working so that, for them, family credit was a 'lifecycle' benefit temporarily topping up income during the lean years of child raising.[42]

However, lone parents tended to settle for a stable pattern of low earnings and claiming.[43] The majority of lone parents on family credit were working part-time over the long term so that, for them, family credit was a long-term wage supplement. They tended to receive large amounts, and although they were not the majority of claimants, they took a high proportion of total family credit expenditure. As Jane Millar and her colleagues put it, couples combine 'work and welfare' while lone mothers combine 'welfare and work'.[44]

Working families tax credit is structurally very similar to family credit and, therefore, likely to have similar effects both on couples and lone parents. The Government, however, appears to have taken little notice of the authoritative findings of the DSS/PSI studies.

Usually, when a Government imposes policies which disregard the known facts it is because their ideological beliefs prevent them from embracing the truth. Despite its efforts to present itself as moderate, pragmatic and non-doctrinaire, the Blair Government nonetheless has made a number of ideological assumptions which have influenced its welfare reforms.

The Underlying Assumptions of New Labour

The Government presents its approach to welfare reform as a 'third way'. In the green paper three alternatives are described: first, 'a privatised future with the welfare state becoming a residual safety net for the poorest and most marginalised'; second, 'the status quo but with more generous and costly benefits'; or the Government's third way, 'promoting opportunity instead of dependence, with the welfare state for the broad mass of people, but in new ways to fit the modern world'.[45]

The Government is anxious to distance itself from the 'old left' view that the welfare problem can be solved just by raising benefits. However, this preference for increasing benefits is not the most disturbing aspect of old-left doctrine. Rather, it is the theory of the human condition that underlies it. It pictures society as made up of individuals who are largely victims of circumstance. They are 'victim-voters' and the political task is to win their votes by promising to use political power to benefit them. In such a society, the influence of the political process is expected to be pervasive.

The counter view—caricatured by the Blair Government as offering a bare safety net and no more—sees human societies as made up of independent characters capable of overcoming adversity and changing their circumstances for the better. The fundamental building blocks of a society are not victim-voters but self-improving, freely co-operating, responsible individuals.

Government spokesmen have occasionally made statements which imply a commitment to welfare reform based on personal responsibility rather than reliance on the state 'from cradle to grave'. When Tony Blair launched the welfare debate at Dudley early in January 1998 he laid down three guiding principles: that anyone in genuine need should be helped; that anyone capable of working should work; and that individuals should provide for themselves when able to do so.[46] However, by the time he came to write the foreword to the green paper in March 1998, the focus on personal responsibility had been weakened. He referred only to: 'work for those who can; security for those who cannot'.[47]

New Labour is different from the 'old left' which typically regarded any talk of holding individuals responsible as an excuse for the callous disregard of their problems. According to the old left, personal responsibility was nothing but the cry of the harsh and uncaring.[48] For them problems such as poverty or unemployment were caused by 'the system' and to attribute any personal responsibility was to divert attention from the real underlying causes. These ideas appealed strongly to class-war enthusiasts.

When Mr Blair suggested that people should provide for themselves, New Labour seemed to be rejecting this doctrine. However, New Labour's commitment to work is not so much driven by a philosophical conversion, but by a pragmatic recognition that it will not be possible to increase public expenditure on services such as health and education unless the able bodied go to work and increase the total taxable income available to the Chancellor.

New Labour has certainly abandoned class-war rhetoric, but still retains a strong reluctance to attribute responsibility to people who are out of work. Its advocates still regard human behaviour primarily as the result of external forces acting upon individuals who are powerless to resist. For this reason they assume that the unemployed all want to work but are prevented from doing so by barriers. It is the task of government to remove the barriers and to 'make work pay'. Consequently, strong elements of the victim-voter theory remain.

So far, two guiding ideas have been identified. The first is the theory that individuals should work to create economic growth to allow tax revenue to be increased without increasing tax rates. The second is the belief that the conditions in which people find themselves are largely the result of outside forces and not primarily the consequence of their earlier behaviour and attitudes. Of course, these are not mutually exclusive alternatives and New Labour does not deny all personal responsibility in the manner of the old left. It does not, for example, make excuses for fraud. Nonetheless, its theory of causation remains close to the determin-istic end of the continuum.

The Government's attachment to this qualified determinism has weakened its capacity to solve the welfare problem. The first page of the green paper lists the three key problems of the present system: first, 'inequality and social exclusion are worsening'; second, 'people face a series of barriers to paid work'; and third, 'fraud is taking money out of the system and away from genuine claimants'.

The last problem is defined in pragmatic terms: money lost to fraudsters cannot be spent on needy pensioners, but it does assume a degree of personal responsibility for wrongdoing. The old left view has typically been that people are driven to fraud by their desperate circumstances. Moreover, the old left often sought to divert attention from the problem by arguing that it was unfair to focus on fraud by the poor when there was business and commercial fraud.

The manner of stating the first two problems of the current system—'social exclusion' and 'barriers'—implies a degree of social determinism. Indeed the term social exclusion has become more central to the Government's rhetoric as time has passed—it has even established a Social Exclusion Unit.

Moreover, the frequent references to social exclusion reflect a third influence on Government policy: a desire to redistribute to 'the deserving poor'. New Labour came under strong attack by socialist academics for abandoning redistribution, not least when over 50 social-policy professors wrote to the *Financial Times* during the Labour Party conference in October 1997. The Govern-ment's policies so far do not suggest any return to the old egalitar-ian agenda, but there is a desire to redistribute to groups classifi-able as 'deserving'. No one in the Government would use any such term now that 'social exclusion' is the preferred label, but in practice two main groups have been classified as deserving of redistribution in their favour. First, people on low incomes who cannot be expected to work are entitled to bigger cash transfers, including the elderly (who have already done their bit). And second, people who work but receive only a low income. An able-bodied person who does not work, however, is no longer considered to be a deserving recipient of higher benefits.

It became clear during the 1998 Budget debate that a fourth element was influencing welfare reform: anti-family social engineering. Elements within the Government contend that the husband/wife family is a condition in which women are dependent on men and that the aim of public policy should be to eradicate this dependency. It is to be ended either by encouraging men and women living as couples to be equal carers and breadwinners, or by subsidising the cost of childcare to allow women and children to live alone without a man. As Melanie Phillips has described, the Government is guided by a belief in 'gender equalisation'.[49] No differences between men and women can be acknowledged. In her speech on the Budget in March 1998, Harriet Harman (then Social Security Secretary) asserted that: 'Women do not view themselves just as dependants of their partners. And this modernising government will not treat them as such.'[50] To underline her wider agenda Ms Harman pointed out that it will not just be the lowest earners who benefit from the childcare tax credit under working families tax credit. 'A lone parent with two children under 11', she said, 'could still be eligible for some childcare tax credit even if her income reached £30,000 a year'. Her departure from office has not diminished the Government's hostility to the traditional family.

Anthony Giddens' book, *The Third Way*, provides further insight into New Labour's approach to the family. Giddens does not like the old social democratic view that the proliferation of family forms is desirable and unproblematic and he quotes Sara McLanahan's work on the harmful effects of family breakdown on children. However, recapturing the traditional family, says Giddens, is a 'non-starter', not least because the traditional family was based on inequality between the sexes and legal ownership of wives by their husbands. Women, he says, were chattels until well into the twentieth century. Children used to be the *raison d'être* of marriage, whereas today they are no longer an economic benefit but rather a major economic cost.[51]

He goes on to ask what ideal we should aim for. His answer is that 'first and most fundamentally' we should aim for equality between the sexes. He goes on: 'There is only one story to tell about the family today, and that is of democracy.'[52] Just as the political process involves formal equality, individual rights, public discussion without violence, and 'authority which is negotiated rather than given by tradition', so should the family.[53] Parents, he concedes, will still claim authority over children, but it 'will be more negotiated and open than before'. He adds that these qualities have exactly the same purchase in homosexual relationships.[54]

Then, only a page after arguing that equality between the sexes is 'first and fundamental,' he says: 'The protection and care of children is the single most important thread that should guide family policy'.[55] He fails to deal with the possibility that the pursuit of equality between the sexes may be incompatible with the interests of children. These contradictions make Giddens not only an ambiguous writer but also a pernicious one. His apparent concessions to other views give his work an air of compromise, but the final proposals he makes are not consistent with what we have learnt about the best methods of raising children.

He advocates a contract of obligation to children, but opposes marriage, which is just such a contract. In reality he gives priority to equalising the caring and earning roles of males and females within marriage at the expense of their children. And he gives priority to the interests of parents, at least one of whom may be happier as a result of a divorce, at the expense of their children. To insist that their obligations continue after divorce ignores the immense practical difficulties of being a good parent without being under the same roof, as confirmed by McLanahan's work which he concedes draws on the 'most exhaustive set of studies carried out to date'.[56] She found that the outcomes for children whose absent father paid maintenance were less harmful than the outcomes for children whose fathers paid nothing, but the results were substantially better when fathers lived with their children.[57]

The proportion of children born outside marriage, says Giddens, probably will not fall and lifelong sexual partnerships will be less common. Consequently, the contractual commitment to a child should be separated from marriage and made a binding matter of law with unmarried and married fathers having the same obligations. Moreover, he can see no reason why childminding and out-of-school care should not be just as available for non-resident fathers as for single mothers. Absent fathers, he says, should have greater rights and be provided with the means to discharge them.[58] This ambiguity towards the family is reflected in the Government's green paper, *Supporting Families*. There is ambiguity in two senses. First, some individuals, of which Giddens is an example, are in two minds. They can no longer deny that family breakdown is bad for children, but cannot bring themselves to support family life based on marriage. Second, some members of the Government advocate policies intended to support the husband/wife family, whereas others are inspired by ultra-feminist animosity to marriage as a condition in which women are subservient to men. Jack Straw and Tony Blair are the leading examples of the former tendency. Ms Harman was for a time the leader of the latter, and following her demise the role has fallen to Baroness (Margaret) Jay and Patricia Hewitt.

Gordon Brown wants to increase tax revenue and reduce public spending by getting people off welfare and into work. However, his objective is in the process of being subverted by the anti-family social engineering described by Giddens. The outcome will be to undermine the self-sufficiency of the husband/wife family, and thereby increase the number of people who depend on public expenditure. In future, some of the taxpayers' money spent on benefit recipients will be called a tax credit rather than a welfare benefit, or concealed as part of a national childcare strategy, but the result will be to raise public spending, further undermine the husband/wife family, and consequently to prevent Gordon Brown from increasing expenditure on health and education without raising taxes. As Martin Wolf argued in a seminal article in the *Financial Times*,[59] more people may be working but they will not necessarily be making a net addition to total economic output because the public cash transfers they receive to 'make work pay' will be so large (often in excess of their wages).

To sum up: four main influences on the policies of the Blair Government can be identified: the focus on work instead of benefit; the belief that barriers are preventing the workless from working; a commitment to the 'deserving' poor; and anti-family social engineering. Their mutual inconsistency is exemplified by the working families tax credit scheme.

The Likely Impact of Working Families Tax Credit

First, many recipients of working families tax credit will receive more in tax subsidy than they earn, even before allowing for the cost of childcare. In such cases there will be no increase in taxable income for Gordon Brown to exploit. Public spending will be no lower and possibly much higher than before, but it will have been rebranded a tax credit instead of a welfare benefit (but without changing the essential fact that both benefits and tax credits involve taking money from one set of people and giving it to another).

Second, still more family breakdown will be encouraged because public subsidies will make it economically more easy for a lone parent to live without a full-time breadwinner. But making lone parenthood economically more feasible does not make lone parents self-sufficient. For the vast majority of people the only economically viable way of raising children is the husband/wife family in which one partner can be the primary breadwinner and the other the main carer. It does not matter how they divide the responsibilities between them. Usually the partner who can earn the most will work. But, except for a highly-paid minority who can afford a full-time nanny, it is not economically possible for a lone parent (father or mother) to both raise a child and work.

Take the situation of a lone mother with two children under 11. By working as few as 16 hours she will receive £78.50 in working families tax credit. She can earn as much as £90 a week before the benefit is reduced at 55p in the pound. If she works 25 hours a week (the average for lone parents on family credit) at an hourly rate of £3.60 (the average is about £4.00) she would earn £90.00 and receive £78.50 working families tax credit without deduction. Child benefit of £23.25 is extra, producing a total income of £191.75 from a wage of £90.00. There will be no tax to pay. Indeed no family with a wage packet of less than £220 a week will have 'net tax' to pay under the new scheme. Even without allowing for childcare, the cost of benefits exceeds her wages.

With two children she can spend up to £150 a week on childcare and receive 70 per cent (£105) back in credit. Only 30 per cent of working lone parents pay anything for childcare, with an average payment of £33.20 a week, but if the lone mother in our example spends £60 a week she will get back £42. Her disposable income after childcare costs would be £173.75.

The Government is officially satisfied because she is in work; and the anti-family social engineers are happy because her children are cared for by someone else and she is not dependent on a man. But the cost to the Government has increased. If she had stayed on income support (if she was over 18) she would have received £107.55 at 1999/2000 figures. The cost to the public purse under the working families tax credit is £143.75, an increase in public spending of over £36 without any addition to total taxable income.

This is quite apart from the likely behavioural effects of public policy measures which make lone parenthood more economically viable. During the 1980s and 1990s lone parenthood increased rapidly. None of the underlying causes has been diminished by the Government and some have been strengthened. The 1998 Budget slightly reduced the relative advantage of marriage (by reducing the value of the married couple's allowance) and the working families tax credit and the national childcare strategy render lone parenthood economically more attractive. On past experience, we should expect these measures to encourage lone parenthood to increase.

It is not clear whether Gordon Brown has been outmanoeuvred by the anti-family social engineers or whether he shares their animosity to the husband/wife family, but either way the impact of the working families tax credit will be to undermine his principal objective: to increase total taxable income so that he can raise tax revenue without raising tax rates.

The Government has occasionally said that it wishes to go back to Beveridge, but the Beveridge report assumed, not only that all adults capable of working would do so, but also that couples who had children would be committed to each other and their children through marriage. Unless the Government recognises that its own policies are undermining marriage and increasing the attractiveness of economically non-viable lifestyles, it will find that its economic strategy will progressively fail.

A third perverse consequence of the working families tax credit is that it automatically increases benefit dependency. Because of the 55 per cent taper more people will become eligible for the tax credit without any behavioural change on their part. This is because at 70 per cent family credit cuts out at about £240 a week for a couple with two children under 11 receiving the 30-hour credit, whereas if, on the same assumptions, the taper were 55 per cent, benefit would cut out at over £290.[60] Under working families tax credit the cut-out is higher still. In its discussion document the Government acknowledges the problem, arguing that 'Reducing marginal rates for the lowest paid inevitably means that marginal rates will have to rise higher up the income distribution' and raise marginal deduction rates for those who are brought in. It mentions the criticism that some second earners might respond by reducing their hours of work to qualify for tax credit. The Government's defence is that the 'highest priority must be to get one member of workless families into work'. In other words, its priority is to solve the unemployment trap rather than the poverty trap. It then makes a rather extraordinary remark. Those 'facing higher marginal rates—as a result of being brought into WFTC entitlement—will be better off' and, the report continues, 'It is difficult to argue that those earning around £300 a week are entrapped in poverty'.[61] But if it is difficult to argue that they are 'entrapped in poverty' why are they receiving a welfare benefit? If the Government's real concern is worklessness, are there not better methods of tackling it without drawing more people into the welfare net?

As it stands, WFTC will mechanically draw more people into benefit who were previously self-sufficient. Consequently it may increase the willingness to claim benefits and thereby, in the name of 'making work pay', increase benefit dependency.

Before suggesting an alternative in Chapter 4, it will be useful to put the debate in its historical context. As Chapter 2 shows, British governments have grappled with these problems in one form or another for hundreds of years but the present government has learnt little from this long experience.

Conclusion

The character of New Labour is becoming clearer. It is not 'old left' and it is not thinly-veiled Thatcherism. It is a brand of collectivism which continues to see the state as the main agent of change. It might be called 'managerial collectivism'. It has a clearer idea of the limits of government than earlier socialists, hence its toleration of competitive markets. But its commitment to markets is based on a pragmatic desire for economic growth. It is not rooted in Adam-Smith liberalism—a theory based on limited government and personal responsibility.

It continues to rely on deterministic theories of human behaviour and consequently to diminish the importance of personal preferences and attitudes as significant causal factors. New Labour, for instance, is reluctant to say that a person has behaved self-destructively, despite the fact that many of those on low incomes have done just that. To take an extreme example, consider a man of 30 who learnt little at school, has subsequently acquired no skills, who has never held a job for more than a few weeks at a time, and who has fathered an illegitimate child or two. Such a man has behaved foolishly and no solution to his low income can be devised without a significant change of attitude on his part—a transformation which can only come from within. Similarly, an individual who had become demoralised by repeated bad luck in finding a job despite strenuous efforts cannot be helped merely by giving him a financial incentive.

New Labour's determinism and the penchant for behavioural manipulation that flows from it, derives from the old-left view that to attribute personal responsibility to an individual is 'blaming the victim'. Public policies which seek to encourage self-improvement are seen as harsh and punitive, whereas in truth they are based on high expectations. People can change for the better. The philosophical assumption behind Adam-Smith liberalism is that people are fallible but capable of personal reform. By assuming that barriers deter people from working the Government is assuming that no personal reform is necessary. Moreover, defining 'financial disincentives' as barriers has led them to adopt policies intended to 'make work pay' and to be reluctant to impose obligations. But since the problem for many on low incomes is not 'barriers' but a self-destructive attitude, policies to make work pay are unlikely to have the intended effect. Because public policies which give money to people on certain conditions have behavioural effects, then such policies may even make matters worse by replacing out-of-work dependency on income support with a new kind of in-work dependency. It hardly needs to be said that to emphasise the importance of individual attitudes is not to assume that there are no factors beyond individual control. There are many such factors, but even in apparently 'hopeless' situations the qualities the individual brings to a given predicament are always relevant.

2

Changing Attitudes to Poverty
and Independence:
From the Poor Law to Beveridge

The Origins of the Poor Law

THERE have always been some people who are not able or willing to support themselves. The earliest legislative efforts were concerned to control vagrancy and the begging and crime with which it was associated. As early as 1388, Richard II had required any person not capable of self-support to remain in his own locality, and in Tudor times there was a period of intense legislation until 1601. In 1495 Henry VII passed a law requiring beggars not able to work to go to the locality in which they had last lived or were best known. In 1504 a further law required vagrants to go to the place of their birth or where they had last lived for three years and to stop begging. In 1531, under Henry VIII, JPs were required to assign to the 'impotent' person (the genuinely needy) a geographical limit within which they were allowed to beg. If found begging outside the limit, they could be jailed for two days and put in the stocks for one night. If able bodied, they were to be whipped and sent back to their place of birth or the last place they had lived for three years, where they must find work.

These earlier measures do not seem to have worked, leading to legislation in 1536 which for the first time involved public officials in co-ordinating charitable giving. A legal obligation was placed on the senior officers of each corporate town and the churchwardens of every parish to collect voluntary alms to care for the impotent poor and put the able bodied to 'continual labour'.[1]

The concern of the legislators seems to have been to ensure that the genuinely needy were helped without creating a reason for the able bodied to exploit public generosity. Consequently severe penalties were provided for 'sturdy beggars'. They were to be whipped for the first offence, have their right ear cropped on a second offence and executed for a third.

However, vagrancy and crime continued to grow and Edward VI found it necessary in 1547 to pass a new law. The problem was blamed partly on the 'foolish pity and mercy' of those charged with implementation and partly on 'the perverse nature and long accustomed idleness of the persons given to loitering'.[2] It seems that the courts had been reluctant to order execution and so the punishment was reduced to slavery for two years.

In 1550 this Act was repealed and the law of 1531 re-instated as well as a provision that sturdy beggars were to be put to work. Instead of slavery, the punishment for refusal to work was 'chaining and beating'. Then legislation of 1551 revived Henry VIII's severe law of 1536 but sought to establish an administrative system that could cope. In every city, corporate town or parish a book was to be kept listing all householders and all the 'impotent' poor. Two persons were to be appointed to collect cash and make a weekly distribution to the poor. Those in genuine need were to be given the most generous help, but they were expected to perform light work if capable. No one was permitted to beg.

Again, Edward VI's statute does not seem to have been fully implemented and was re-enacted in 1555 by Mary Tudor. This too failed, primarily because many people were reluctant to give money to the parish collectors.

In 1563 Elizabeth I made a further attempt to overcome this reluctance to give alms to the parish. JPs and churchwardens were required to tax reluctant payers at the complaint of the vicar, the churchwardens and the bishop. This too does not seem to have worked and finally in 1572 a regular weekly tax was imposed. The Act also states that England and Wales were 'exceedingly pestered' by 'rogues, vagabonds and sturdy beggars' leading daily to 'horrible murders, thefts and great outrage'. The Act states its intention of preventing a system designed to relieve the genuinely needy from being abused by the able bodied. It sought to ensure that the 'poor, aged and impotent' should be provided for so that they did not need to beg and also to repress 'rogues, vagabonds and sturdy beggars'.[3] The latter would be set to work or, if they persisted in begging, punished by whipping for a first offence, jail for a second and death for third. Royal patience also ran out with those who refused to pay the tax levied by the collectors. They could be jailed until they agreed to pay.

The law of 1572 was not repealed, but in 1598 new punishments were provided for. A wandering person who refused to work and who was unable to support himself was to be 'whipped until his body may be bloody' and sent back to his original parish or last abode where he would be put to work. Anyone refusing to reform his conduct could be sent to the house of correction, the local jail or ultimately transported. The legislation of 1598 hardly differs from the famous 43rd of Elizabeth (1601) which remained the basis of poor law provision until 1834.

The New Poor Law

The operation of the poor laws does not seem to have aroused great controversy until the beginning of the nineteenth century, when law makers once again found themselves grappling with the same problem: that efforts to show decency towards the genuinely destitute were being abused by the able bodied. In 1834 a new remedy was devised without the harshness of the Tudor era.

However, a further transformation was taking place. The Elizabethan poor law had developed during a paternalistic age, when JPs set wages and regulated the movement of people, and this paternalism continued to be a powerful reality until well into the nineteenth century, despite the developing ethos of personal responsibility. Rapid industrialisation and urbanisation during the nineteenth century made these constraints unworkable. Consequently, liberal critics of the old paternalism and the style of poor law that went with it sought a different role for the state which recognised the value of liberty whilst safeguarding the interests of the less fortunate.

By the 1820s and 1830s it was widely recognised that a well-intentioned welfare system had produced what we now call benefit dependency, as well as a large number of fraudulent claims, more births out of wedlock and more crime. A parliamentary select committee had recommended abolition in 1817 but no legislative action was taken until 1834.

Although we think of ourselves as far more advanced, the issues and debates in the 1830s have a strikingly modern resonance, perhaps because dependency had reached similar proportions. In 1997 about 17 per cent of the population relied on income support alone (27 per cent if the other means-tested benefits are included). When Tocqueville visited England in 1833 he estimated that one-sixth (17 per cent) of the population were reliant on poor relief, a much higher proportion than elsewhere in Europe.[4]

As Gertrude Himmelfarb has brilliantly described in her classic, *The Idea of Poverty*, public policy at the time was concerned with encouraging the capacity for independent self-support. The dominant ethos of the age was that the quality of life for individuals would be better if they lived as free and responsible persons. Moreover, such a life was in the common good. Writers at the time were conscious that Britain was undergoing a dramatic change from a social order in which the majority of people lived out their days in a single locality and perhaps worked for a single master to one in which individuals took responsibility for choosing their occupation, locality and style of life. As Macfarlane[5] has shown, there was far more individualism in pre-modern times than has been supposed, but by the second half of the eighteenth century the freedom of the individual was a noticeable reality that was being remarked on by many observers.

Most people welcomed the emerging freedom. The opportunity to find new work or move to a new locality was preferable to tied labour or lifelong work for a harsh employer. But for some the exercise of responsibility was an unwelcome burden. Some individuals could not cope at all, and some not all the time. The emerging issue for public policy was how to give help to those who needed it without encouraging others to abandon the effort to be self-supporting. By the 1830s the folly of undiluted paternalism in public policy had become obvious.

In 1832 a royal commission was appointed to investigate. Its members included Edwin Chadwick and Nassau Senior and its report was published in 1834. Assistant commissioners travelled all around the country and found that cash relief took five main forms:

1. *Relief without labour*—which usually involved the pauper turning up somewhere to prevent him from doing paid work while receiving relief.[6]

2. *Allowances in support of wages*—which were usually paid on a scale as at Speenhamland or Cambridge.[7] In Berkshire and Wiltshire this 'bread money' was a regular payment and a distinction was made between 'bread money' and 'going on the parish', not very different from the present government's distinction between a tax credit and a welfare benefit.[8] In Thaxted, Essex, cash payments were based on the value of half a peck of flour for each individual plus 6d for both parents and 4d per child. If wages did not reach that amount they were made up out of the poor rate. And in an example of 'making work pay' 1830s-style, if a man earned more than 8s he could keep the extra in order not to 'discourage industry'.[9]

3. *The roundsmen or ticket system*—under which individuals were sent to work for various property owners in turn.[10]

4. *Parish employment*—that is, working directly for parish officials. The report found this the least common because it was the most trouble to the parish.[11]

5. *Setting a labour rate*—a system requiring landowners to employ a number of individuals based on the rateable value of their property.[12]

For 100 years or more, the recommendations of the 1834 commissioners have been presented by historians as a harsh crack-down. But the report was written with considerable sympathy for the 'labouring classes'. The commissioners argued against the settlement laws, which they saw as contrivances to keep wages low but, above all, they rejected abolition of the poor law, a course that had been urged by Malthus and many others. It was, said the report, repugnant to common sentiment to allow people to perish, indeed it was repugnant to public opinion to punish crime if it was the only alternative to starvation.[13] The commissioners seem to have shared in this 'common sentiment' and believed that able-bodied people unable to support themselves—the indigent—could 'safely' and 'beneficially' be assisted by means of a legal system of relief.[14] But a public system of relief was defensible only if it was organised according to very strict principles.

The recommendations were based on concrete experience of reform in many parts of the country where the results had been to the lasting benefit of independent labourers, not least because wages had increased.[15] A central concern of the commission was with the quality of life of the great majority. In one sense a pauper's life resembled that of a slave, said the commissioners. Paupers received a lower income but easy work—a slave's security without the risk of punishment.[16] Looking around the country, they found that the happiest people were those reliant on their own exertions for income. They lived as responsible, thinking persons, raised their children with care and contributed to the community.

The commissioners of 1834 tried to distinguish between three groups. First, there were some people who were too ill or frail to earn a living at all. It was accepted without question that they should receive assistance at the public expense. Second, there were people who were able bodied and could normally earn a living but were temporarily unable to do so. They could also receive temporary help from the public purse, so long as it was calculated to encourage an early return to work. Third, there were people capable of work but not able to earn very much. Until 1834 their wages had often been subsidised by the poor law authorities. Here is where the commissioners drew the line. They took the view that, even if a person was only capable of labouring for mere subsistence, to do so was more honourable than relying permanently on others. To supplement wages seemed harmless enough but in practice it had altered the conduct of workers, who did not seize opportunities to earn more and who were inclined to take on commitments they could not meet, particularly having larger families than they could afford. It created habits of what we now call dependency. The commissioners discovered a 'diminishing reluctance to claim an apparent benefit, the receipt of which imposed no sacrifice, except a sensation of shame quickly obliterated by habit'.[17]

There was little sympathy at the time for able-bodied individuals who simply refused to work, but there was much for families whose breadwinner could only command a low wage. The commissioners thought carefully about the predicament of such families and came to two conclusions. First, they should not be shielded from the consequences of their actions to such an extent that they no longer felt responsible. If they could only afford one or two children it was the couple's responsibility to limit their family. Second, they discovered from their investigations that families in which the man was an independent worker, even if on a low income, lived happier and more wholesome lives; whereas families dependent on poor relief tended to live a degraded existence and provided a bad environment for the raising of children. Independence, they concluded, even on a low income was better for the parents, the children and the whole community.

Mere poverty, in the sense of a shortfall between income and expenses, should not be confused with incapacity for self-support. The ambiguity of the word 'poor' had given the impression that anyone with a low income was entitled to a share of public funds, a confusion fostered by the supplementation of wages. Moreover, demands for 'rights' were couched in vague terms such as 'fair', 'reasonable' or 'adequate' which tended to raise expectations such that discontent was often greatest in localities where relief was most generous.[18] In 1830 there had been serious agricultural riots—the Swing riots—and the commission noted that it was almost as if, the more generous the locality, the more serious the discontent, citing Reading and Newbury as examples. But where wages were a matter of contract there was more contentment.[19]

Thus, the practice of paying poor relief to men in work had blurred the boundary between independence and dependence. Every person, the commissioners believed, should reap the reward of his own prudence and hard work, and pay the price of mistakes. A policy of open-ended subsidy undermined the natural consequences of human conduct. The effect of the poor laws was 'to repeal *pro tanto* the law of nature by which the effects of each man's improvidence or misconduct are borne by himself and his family', and by the same token 'to repeal *pro tanto* the law by which each man and his family enjoy the benefit of his own prudence and virtue'.[20]

Consequently, wage subsidisation and unconditional relief had produced harmful effects on character. Knowing that their well-being did not depend on their exertions, some workers had become idle and dissolute and ultimately 'callous to their own degradation'.[21] Moreover, wages had been lowered by irresponsible employers, and this had in turn lowered the wages for the workers of independent character, making their lot harder still. The evidence was that, once this process began, the deterioration tended to spread.

To end the progressive degradation of the independent labourer, the commissioners sought to create a 'broad line of distinction between the class of independent labourers and the class of paupers'.[22] This end was to be accomplished by making the lot of the able-bodied pauper less attractive—'less eligible' in the famous phrase of the commission—than that of the independent worker. It was only by 'making relief in all cases less agreeable than wages', they said, 'that any thing deserving the name of improvement can be hoped for'.[23] The distinction was to be maintained by aiding the able-bodied pauper only in the workhouse, except for medical relief. Here food, shelter, work and discipline would be regulated to encourage an early return to independence.

Fundamental to their thinking was the stipulation that individuals would enter the workhouse by choice. There would be no test of their means or merit. If they applied for relief on workhouse terms, they would be provided with a sufficient diet and clean accommodation, but subject to work and discipline. If they preferred that to an independent life, so be it. The test was 'self acting'. By applying for aid, the individual crossed the line between pauperism and independence.[24]

Although the system has been described by historians as harsh, it was humane in its intentions and certainly more humane in practice than earlier laws which had provided for whipping and transportation.

The commissioners were inspired by the ideal of a society of free and responsible individuals in which each family took pains to be self-sufficient so that its members could make a positive contribution to the life of the community. Among the tasks of the wider community was to help the less fortunate, but hard experience had taught that an uncomfortably large number of people responded to the availability of help by refraining from work and living at the expense of others. But the remedy was not to withdraw help altogether. Rather it was to give help wisely. The natural result of not working was starvation to death, but the commissioners sought to be 'kinder than nature' by maintaining a safety net without entirely removing the consequences of unwise behaviour. They did not want to encourage idleness by paying able-bodied persons whether they worked or not; but rather than offer potential idlers a choice between work or starvation they presented them with a choice between independent work or residence in the workhouse environment of wholesome food and accommodation combined with the discipline of work.

The Report has been presented as a centralising measure by many historians.[25] But the commissioners opposed a national scheme because they believed that, if the government promised subsistence to all, it would make matters even worse.[26] Moreover, local experimentation had enabled them to discover the remedy they ultimately recommended. Consequently, they advocated a system guided by a central board but with local discretion. The intention was for the board to enforce what today would be called 'best practice' rather than to assume full central control.

The Report based its recommendations on the experience of localities where reforms had already been introduced following earlier criticism, including Swallowfield (Berks) where relief was restricted to five-sixths of the normal wage,[27] Welwyn (Herts),[28] St Mary in Nottingham, and Uley in Gloucester, where able-bodied paupers were given wholesome food but 'irksome' work.[29] In particular, the payment of relief only in the workhouse had already been implemented successfully in Llangaddock in Brecon and Leckhamstead in Berks.[30]

As liberals with high expectations of the common person, they took a few sideswipes at the paternalistic upper-crust administrators of the poor law, noting that administrators who distinguished themselves as reformers had usually risen from the labouring classes.[31] And they pointed out that, in reforming districts, pauperism had fallen without any increase in hardship. Indeed the standard of living of labourers had risen. In Cookham (Berks) the number of paupers had fallen by 63 and none moved out of the area.[32] In Swallowfield there had been a 50 per cent fall.[33]

In Leckhamstead, where relief was given on workhouse terms alone, the number of paupers had fallen from 43 to three, out of a total population of 499.[34] In Southwell the number of paupers had fallen from 80 to 11.[35]

The commissioners were convinced from experience in these reforming districts that the lot of the ordinary labourer would be much improved by their recommendations.[36] Wages had increased at White Waltham, Cookham, Hatfield and Welwyn.[37] This, said the commission, was because workers performed better, increasing the capital of employers, who then paid higher wages in their turn.[38] No less important, improvident marriages and illegitimacy had been reduced and crime had fallen.[39] Able-bodied pauperism, said the commissioners, was often the result of indolence and vice and could be avoided by 'ordinary care and industry'—habits which were all too easily undermined by thoughtless giving.[40]

The theory of human nature which guided the commission is exemplified by the attention paid to before-and-after examples of individuals whose lives had been transformed for the better in reforming districts. Fifteen examples are given from Swallowfield. Typical was the story of Charles Cordery, a married man with four children who was a 'skilful and diligent' workman:

> under the former system, he was almost always dependent upon the parish; his wife and children were as idle and ragged as himself; and so bad was their character for pilfering and depredation, that they were successively turned out of every cottage that was occupied by them. At last they were absolutely without a roof to shelter them, and the vestry refused to support them any longer out of the rates.

A Mr Russell took pity on them and gave them a cottage. He told the commission that, without the prospect of poor relief, Mr Cordery had subsequently been in constant work, his family in comfort and his rent regularly paid.[41]

The reforms of 1834 reflected the new climate of opinion that had led to the return of a Whig Government under Lord Grey in 1831. His administration promptly enacted the Reform Act of 1832 to widen the franchise, and the Poor Law Amendment Act of 1834. Edwin Chadwick summed up the new mood of hostility to paternalism and confidence in human creativity. He described how the upper classes had sought to help the poor through charities and profuse expenditure financed from the rates which, he thought, had proved 'the most potent means of retarding the improvement of the labouring population'. The best way for the wealthy to help the poor would be 'in acting with the labouring classes rather than for them' by enabling them to act for themselves through organisations such as provident institutions.[42]

In keeping with this spirit, a new Friendly Societies Act was also passed in 1834 to encourage mutual aid associations. Before 1834, JPs had been required to satisfy themselves that new societies were desirable and that there was not already another society fulfilling the same need, a measure that discouraged competition and the improvements it tended to bring. The 1834 Act removed this restriction. Prior to 1834 JPs had also to be satisfied that the rules of a society were 'fit and proper', but after the Act the government barrister (later the Registrar) had only to be satisfied that rules were 'in conformity with law'. JPs were formerly empowered to establish that the tables of contributions and benefits had been approved by two actuaries or persons skilled in calculation. This requirement was abolished and the aims of friendly societies were widened to include any lawful purpose. This liberal framework of law allowed people to band together to meet their own needs through mutual organisations as they believed best. The rise and significance of these mutual aid associations is described in my earlier book, *Reinventing Civil Society*.

The Poor Law at the End of the Nineteenth Century

The principles of 1834 were not fully implemented in every locality and debate about the best method of assisting the poor continued. By the end of the century there was a recognisably different consensus. Among the clearest statements of the prevailing view at the beginning of the twentieth century was that of Majority Report of the 1909 Royal Commission on the Poor Laws. The main author of the Majority Report was Helen Bosanquet of the Charity Organisation Society. She wrote several articles and a book describing her underlying philosophy.[43]

In every country there were people, she said, who for one reason or another were without the necessities of life. In England, the legal responsibility for self-support lay in the first place upon each individual, if capable; in the second upon the family; and failing both upon the taxpayers.[44] Helen Bosanquet upheld the principle of a public duty to help:

> no greater blow could be struck at the feeling of unity which holds a community together than that a part of it should be allowed to perish for want while another part could have assisted and did not.[45]

But to say as much was just the start: 'a community owes much more to its members than the mere maintenance of life; and it is by aiming so low that it achieves such deplorable results'.[46] True respect should involve making demands. We cannot grow as people without a struggle to overcome difficulties. Consequently, thoughtless help, she said, could make matters worse. In particular, some people neglect relationships that would allow them to ask for help in a spirit of mutual respect: they allow friendships to wither, or neglect family ties, and fail to join organisations where help could be found.

She faced squarely the unavoidable side-effect of any system of government relief. The very fact of its existence caused 'many to fail who might otherwise have succeeded' in their duty of self-support.[47] The problem of public assistance was, therefore, to offer help, 'in such a way as to diminish rather than to increase the number of those requiring it'.[48] She did not favour the policy of simple deterrence recommended in 1834, but believed that the test of a good policy was:

> the degree of success which it achieves in combining a policy which shall not encourage laziness and self-indulgence with one which shall be really remedial in the assistance afforded. It fails when it is attractive to the profligate, but it fails no less when it is deterrent to those who might be restored by its services to health and independence.[49]

The poor law as it stood in 1909 aimed at deterrence but it had failed.[50] She emphasised the diversity of those who needed assistance:

> The population which comes within the scope of the Poor Law is made up of the most heterogeneous elements. Individuals of every age, of every shade of character, of every degree of physical or moral

incapacity, with every variety of disease or disability, are all brought together by the one common fact that they demand to be maintained at the cost of the community.[51]

No society can simply pay anyone who asks—and so someone must decide whether or not to assist and what form the assistance should take.

We should always, she said, 'lend a hand to our brother in his difficulties', but giving money was not the key.[52] The economic position of any individual is, she argues, so dependent upon 'qualities which are not primarily or obviously economic' that we will only discover the best method of improving the economic position of the people if we enlist 'the whole mind and interests of the people in question'.[53]

The Majority Report did not maintain that deficiencies of character were always and necessarily the problem: 'There are some who are physically or morally incapable of independence under any administration; and there are many who are not to be tempted from it by anything less than sheer necessity'.[54] However, there were also many people who 'simply follow the line of least resistance'. For these people on 'the borderland' an unwise policy of relief on easy terms was fatal: 'they quickly lose the habits of energy and foresight, and become in the true sense of the word pauperised'.[55]

The Gradual Weakening of Personal Responsibility During the Twentieth Century

Towards the end of the nineteenth century the ethos of personal responsibility celebrated by Helen Bosanquet had begun to come under attack, especially by intellectuals who preferred to analyse human behaviour as if it were a response to scientific laws. They gave scant attention to the personal qualities and attitudes of the individual. As the great twentieth century philosophers of liberty, Popper and Hayek, have argued, these scientific theories—particularly those claiming to understand the iron laws of history—reinforced the authoritarian political movements, such as Italian fascism, Nazism and Russian communism, that came to prominence. In their extreme forms these doctrines did not catch on in Britain but they came to influence our self-understanding and to permeate intellectual life at all levels. Poverty was prominent among the economic and social phenomena that came to be explained by theories that diminished the importance of personal responsibility.

The 'Poverty Line'

The concern of policy makers after 1834 had been to establish the line between independence and dependence, whereas the central concern of the new generation of social analysts at the end of the nineteenth century was to establish a poverty line and to measure how many were below it, whether in work or not. They lost sight of the earlier belief that self-sufficiency through work, even on a low income, was preferable to dependence on the work of others. The studies of writers such as Charles Booth and B.S. Rowntree implied that the problem was a shortage of money that could be overcome by giving people more. In her book, *The Strength of the People*, Helen Bosanquet criticised the new tendency to treat those below the 'poverty line' as incapable of self-support. We 'manufacture' our poor by 'our crude belief that the Poverty Line is a question of money, and that by merely putting money or money's worth into a man's hands we can raise him above it' and by our 'ignorant meddling which robs human lives of far more than we give in return'.[56]

The use of the term 'poverty line' restored credibility to the 'mischievous ambiguity of the word poor', which had been criticised by the 1834 commission. To speak of a poverty line failed to explain the causes of low income. In particular, it failed to distinguish between people who had a low income because they were not capable of self-sufficiency; people who were in work but on a low income; and individuals who were able bodied but abstaining from work. Moreover, the idea of a poverty line lent itself to exaggeration. Charles Booth produced statistics for East London as well as the whole of the capital. When he studied the whole of London, Booth had divided the population into eight classes (A-H). He found that class A (loafers and petty criminals) comprised 0.9 per cent, class B (the 'very poor') 7.5 per cent and classes C and D (the poor) 22.3 per cent. Altogether that meant that 30.7 per cent of the population of London was classified as 'in poverty' and 69.3 per cent 'in comfort'.[57] This was the basis of the alarmist claim at the time that one-third of the population of the capital was in poverty.

However, Booth by no means advocated a simplistic approach to reform and retained much of the moral concern of earlier reformers. Initially he had studied 900,000 people in East London only. Those in class A, about 11,000 people, were the lowest class of 'loafers' and petty criminals. Class B (the 'very poor') contained 100,000 persons, about 11 per cent of the population studied. They lived largely on casual earnings and were at all times more or less 'in want'.[58] Booth looked upon them as 'helpless and incompetent' and urged that they be put under the tutelage of the state:

> Put practically... my suggestion is that these people should be given an opportunity to live as families in industrial groups, planted wherever land and building materials were cheap; being well housed, well fed, and well warmed; and taught, trained, and employed from morning to night on work, indoors or out, for themselves or on Government account; in the building of their own dwellings, in the cultivation of land, in the making of clothes, or in the making of furniture.[59]

They would be 'servants of the State', who would have wages credited to them at a 'fair and proportionate rate'. If they did not work well enough they would go to the workhouse where they would be unable to live as a family; but if they worked well they could go out into the outside world again as free persons. Careful provision for children would be made: 'incompetence need not be hereditary'.[60] This 'limited Socialism', as he called it, would mean that the undesirables in class A would be no longer confounded with 'the unemployed' and 'gradually harried out of existence'. Class B 'would be cared for, and its children given fair chances'.[61] Perhaps most important of all, the absence of competition from members of class B would enable the 'respectable' working classes C and D) to earn higher wages and thus more easily raise themselves by their own endeavours.

There were about 200,000 people in classes C and D. Members of these classes were not 'in want', according to Booth, but he called them 'the poor' because 'they would be much the better for more of everything'. This was a use of language that did not assist clear interpretation.[62] In the whole of London 8.4 per cent of the population constituted the main problem (classes A and B) and even in East London, with its concentration of casual labourers, classes A and B comprised only 12.3 per cent of the population.

Thus, Booth himself did not diminish the importance of personal responsibility, though his estimate of the poverty line was used by those who did.

The second pioneer of the modern poverty study was B.S. Rowntree. He conducted three surveys in York: in 1899, 1936 and 1950. The 1899 survey distinguished between 'primary' and 'secondary' poverty. Primary poverty was described as: 'Families whose total earnings are insufficient to obtain the minimum necessaries for the maintenance of merely physical efficiency'. Secondary poverty was: 'Families whose total earnings would be sufficient for the maintenance of merely physical efficiency were it not that some portion of it is absorbed by other expenditure, either useful or wasteful'.[63]

He found in 1899 that 10 per cent of the population of York was in 'primary poverty'. He also calculated a figure for 'secondary poverty' in 1899, to allow comparison with Booth's 30.7 per cent. Rowntree's estimate for York was 28 per cent, which played into the hands of political groups intent on exaggeration to justify extending the power of the state over economic and social conditions.

The Legislative Origins of Benefit Dependency

Legislation followed the return of a new government in 1906— ironically a Liberal government with little understanding of liberal principles. In 1908 non-contributory pensions were introduced. By 1909 about 500,000 people were in receipt of pensions under the 1908 Act, many of whom might previously have relied on poor relief.

Other legislation also introduced new state benefits. The 1911 National Insurance Act introduced sick pay and, under Part II, unemployment insurance for 2.25 million employees. Unemployment benefit was extended in 1916 to another 1.5 million, and the Unemployment Insurance Act of 1920 extended it to 11 million people altogether.[64]

Initially, unemployment insurance was widely supported because it seemed to be consistent with the ethos of self-sufficiency. Anyone could be unfortunate enough to be thrown out of work and it was a wise precaution to be insured. A person who claimed unemployment benefit was not asking for poor relief but reaping the reward of his earlier prudence in insuring himself. However, unemployment insurance was never established on actuarially sound principles. Even before the 1920 Act was passed, discretionary payments were made in contradiction of strict insurance principles. In 1918 the military out-of-work donation was paid to servicemen who did not have a job after demobilisation. It was followed by an extended benefit scheme for those who had not worked long enough to qualify for unemployment benefit. In effect, by 1921 benefit had become a 'right', ostensibly justified because it was 'insurance' when, in reality, sufficient insurance contributions had not been paid. In 1927 'transitional benefit' was introduced, initially as a temporary measure to be cancelled in 1929, but it was extended until the establishment of the Unemployment Assistance Board in 1934.

The Unemployment Assistance Board took responsibility for the unemployed who did not qualify for insurance from January 1935 and relaxed qualifying conditions still further. In 1937 a further 100,000 persons, previously the responsibility of the public assistance committees, were taken on by the Unemployment Assistance Board. (In 1929 the poor law guardians had been abolished and local authorities had been required to establish public assistance committees to assume their responsibilities.)

Further relaxation followed in 1941. Until that year public assistance for the able-bodied unemployed not entitled to insurance was subject to a means test that took into account the resources of the whole household. However, the Determination of Needs Act, 1941, replaced it with a means test which took into account only the resources of the applicant, the applicant's wife or husband and any dependants. The actual income of non-dependants (such as lodgers or grown-up children still living at home) was disregarded but they were assumed to contribute 7s a week, subject to a sliding scale.[65]

In 1925 the Widows', Orphans', and Old Age Contributory Pensions Act had been introduced, the first national scheme of contributory pensions (the 1908 scheme was means-tested and financed from general taxes). The benefits were not paid for by the contributions and came into force in three stages. From January 1926, there were pensions of 10*s* (50p) a week for widows. From July 1926, old age pensions of 10*s* a week were paid to persons over the age of 70. And from January 1928, pensions of 10*s* a week were paid to insured persons aged between 65 and 70. Henceforward, all insured men reaching the age of 65, as well as their wives, were to receive pensions.

The 1940 Old Age and Widows' Pensions Act provided that, from July 1940, the old age pension of 10s a week should be payable from the age of 60, instead of 65, to an insured woman or the wife of an insured man who had reached the age of 65. This Act also introduced supplementary pensions for needy old-age pensioners and widow pensioners over the age of 60. The responsibility for supplementary pensions was placed on the Unemployment Assistance Board, which was renamed the Assistance Board.[66]

Beveridge

Thus, most elements of the post-war welfare state were already in place by the time of the Beveridge report of 1942. However, despite Beveridge's keen awareness of the dangers of benefit dependency, the reforms of the 1940s still further entrenched the role of government and undermined personal responsibility.

Studies of poverty conducted in the 1930s strongly influenced Beveridge. By 1936 Rowntree had abandoned efforts to calculate secondary poverty because he believed there was no reliable way of estimating it.[67] Using the 1899 measure of 'primary poverty', he found only four per cent below the line in 1936.[68] In that year he also used a higher 'primary' standard to take account of additional items such as newspapers, tobacco and beer. Against that higher standard he found 18 per cent in poverty. (In 1950, also using the higher 1936 standard, he found only two per cent in poverty.)

Despite his focus on the 'poverty line'—and unlike later poverty analysts—Rowntree did not fall into the trap of explaining poverty as if it were entirely the result of outside forces. He thought that primary poverty was the result of lifecycle change. The life of the labourer, he had said in 1899, comprised 'five alternating periods of want and comparative plenty'.[69] During early childhood he might be in poverty until his brothers or sisters were able to contribute to the family income. Then came a period of plenty when he was earning but living with his parents, a period that continued into marriage until children came along. During this period it was essential to save in preparation for raising children. The third phase was a period of want which followed the arrival of children until they were old enough to earn. Then followed a period of plenty after the children began to earn, continuing after they had left home until retirement. In old age a period of want might follow if savings were insufficient. Thus, said Rowntree, the 7,230 persons who had been in primary poverty in York in 1899 'represent merely that section who happened to be in one of these poverty periods at the time the inquiry was made'. Many, he said, 'will, in the course of time, pass on into a period of comparative prosperity'.[70]

He did not shrink from identifying human folly as among the causes of poverty and compared the age at which skilled workers and unskilled labourers married in 1898 and 1899. Nearly one-third of the labourers married when they were under 23 years of age, while less than one-fifth of the skilled workers did so; and 58 per cent of the labourers married under the age of 26, compared with 49 per cent of the skilled workers.[71] Marrying young reduced the time available for saving in preparation for the lean years of raising children.

His classification was similar in the 1930s, although by then he was referring to the 'three periods of economic stress': childhood, parenthood before children begin to earn, and old age. However, by the 1930s personal responsibility played a diminished part in his explanation. Three-quarters of the families with no bread-winner in work lived on benefits and, he said, their poverty could 'be remedied by raising the benefits'.[72] For those in work, the solution was more complex but he advocated a minimum wage and income-tested allowances for children.[73]

Beveridge took the view, based on the 1930s poverty surveys by Rowntree and others, that from three-quarters to five-sixths of want was due to the interruption of earnings and that the remaining one-quarter to one-sixth was due to failure to relate income to the size of the family.[74] That is, Beveridge assumed that most people, most of the time, would be in work and self-supporting and that the main problem was the interruption of earnings through ill-health or unemployment. National insurance was, therefore, intended to tide people over until they got back on their feet, or to provide for people who were permanently incapacitated or too old to work.

To deal with the minority—a quarter to one-sixth—whose income was insufficient for their family size (Rowntree's lifecycle poverty) Beveridge proposed child allowances.[75] This recommendation was a departure from the view of earlier thinkers, who believed that having children was the responsibility of parents. Beveridge, however, saw children in more collectivist terms as part of his plan to pay for pensions. He was worried that the low reproduction rate of the British would undermine the insurance basis of his plan as the proportion of elderly people increased. Unless the reproduction rate were to be 'raised very materially in the near future,' said the report, 'a rapid and continuous decline of the population cannot be prevented'. This fact made it 'imperative to give first place in social expenditure to the care of childhood and to the safeguarding of maternity'.[76]

As we have seen, personal responsibility was weakened by Rowntree and had an influence on public policy through Beveridge, but both Rowntree and Beveridge still took it for granted that the great majority of people would be self-sufficient through work and Beveridge was aware that measures to deal with the 'workshy' were necessary.[77] We can say with justice that, between them, Rowntree and Beveridge brought about a weakening of personal responsibility but not its abandonment. It was not until the 1960s that intellectuals began to cast it aside in its entirety.

The final paragraph of Rowntree's *Poverty and Progress*, completed in 1941 when Britain was fighting for its life against Hitler, sounded a warning:

> Everywhere democracy is challenged. A totalitarian State does not demand high intellectual or spiritual standards from its people; on the contrary it can only function successfully when they cease to think for themselves and are willing to obey the command to worship false gods. But a democratic State can only flourish if the

level of intelligence of the community is high and its spiritual life dynamic.[78]

Rowntree plainly retained some understanding that material conditions played only a part in creating a good society but like so many of his generation he did not see that his own measures substituted action by the state for action by the individual, thus reducing the occasions on which people had to 'think for themselves'—the very criterion that, in his own view, distinguished a free people from the masses in a totalitarian state.

Rowntree, however, had little in common with the modern egalitarian. His concern was to define the minimum on which someone could reasonably be expected to live and to measure over time how many were above or below the line. Even though the line was raised, by the 1950s he accurately reported that few people were in poverty. Later analysts had no such scruples, as I will show below.

3

The Rise and Decline of
Egocentric Collectivism

The Rediscovery of Poverty

ROWNTREE'S final survey of 1950 found only two per cent in poverty using the higher 1936 measure and his manner of perceiving the poverty line as a minimum was predominant until the early 1960s, when a very different kind of argument began to be applied. From that time, some writers began to use statistics more as a call to action against 'the system'. In their view there was 'structural poverty' and the system itself was at fault. It followed that, if poverty was structural, it could not be attributed to individuals. Thus, no one could be responsible for his own predicament and to assert the importance of personal responsibility was to 'blame the victim'. In America Michael Harrington's *The Other America* led the way in putting this argument, claiming in 1962 that about 50 million people were 'poor' in the United States.[1]

Harrington was not particularly careful about the facts he deployed. In the appendix to his book, where authors usually describe the scrupulousness of their research methods, he said: 'If my interpretation is bleak and grim, and even if it overstates the case slightly, that is intentional'. My moral point of departure, he said, 'is a sense of outrage, a feeling that the obvious and existing problem of the poor is so shocking that it would be better to describe it in dark tones rather than to minimise it.'[2] This attitude was later described by American sociologist, Christopher Jencks, as 'lying for justice'. Harrington also deployed the language of 'exclusion' that was to feature so prominently in later years:

> The American poor are not poor in Hong Kong or in the sixteenth century; they are poor here and now, in the United States. They are dispossessed in terms of what the rest of the nation enjoys... They

live on the fringe, the margin. They watch the movies and read the magazines of affluent America, and these tell them that they are internal exiles.[3]

It is this 'sense of exclusion', he said, that intensifies the pessimism of the poor and 'intensifies the exclusion'.[4] Poverty, he argued:

> should be defined psychologically in terms of those whose place in the society is such that they are internal exiles who, almost inevitably, develop attitudes of defeat and pessimism and who are therefore excluded from taking advantage of new opportunities.[5]

Harrington's book is widely reputed to have sparked the US 'War on Poverty', one of the great public-policy catastrophes of all time.

In the UK the nearest equivalent to *The Other America* was *The Poor and the Poorest* by Peter Townsend and Brian Abel Smith, published in 1965.[6] They abandoned Rowntree's efforts to identify a 'sufficiency' of income and defined the poverty line as 140 per cent of the basic national assistance scale plus rent and/or other housing costs. They found that nearly 18 per cent of households were in poverty, some 7.5 million people including 2.25 million children.[7] The tone of the study was not as emotive as Harrington's and it did not lead to a UK 'war on poverty'. However, it was instrumental in the formation of the Child Poverty Action Group, which was subsequently to campaign for higher welfare benefits.

The high point of animosity to personal responsibility was probably reached in the 1970s. By then the prevailing orthodoxy had come to embrace a paradoxical combination of ideas which might be called 'egocentric collectivism'. Four elements can be distinguished. First, it rested on an interpretation of the human condition that emphasised individual powerlessness. To hold people responsible was, as argued earlier, to 'blame the victim'. The implication of this view was that the pressing political task was to transfer funds to the helpless section of the population—the 'victim-voters', comprising the poor or the working class.

Second, many, but not all, collectivists were egalitarians who were not content to transfer cash to 'the poor' but sought in addition to use the power of the state to equalise incomes and wealth.

Third, egocentric collectivists emphasised individual claims on other members of the society—there were universal 'welfare rights' with no corresponding obligations. This attitude is closely associated with a tendency to regard all collective action as political action. During the nineteenth-century high point of Adam-Smith liberalism, people who were concerned about an issue organised a committee to solve it directly. They knew the importance of maintaining a vigorous civil society. At the high point of egocentric collectivism in the 1970s, the popular instinct was to organise a 'demo' and demand political action. Individuals saw themselves as part of a mass society on which they could make demands. By contrast, in the tradition of Adam-Smith liberalism individuals were custodians of an inherited culture, to be upheld and developed as circumstances demanded, and they were possessors of personal gifts and talents which could be improved or neglected and used for good or ill at their discretion. To use a trivial parallel, under egocentric collectivism individuals had become more like spectators at a sporting spectacle rather than players of sport making their individual and unique contribution to the team.

Fourth, and closely related to this diminishing of the individual in a mass society, there was an element of cultural nihilism—we should be released from all restraints, whether moral, cultural or legal.

As Norman Dennis has shown, the ultimate intellectual origins of 1960s and 1970s collectivism lay in Marxist hostility towards capitalism and its desire to tear it down by making impossible demands.[8] However, the version of this doctrine that predominated in the United States, advocated most prominently by Michael Harrington, was hostile to 'the system' but did not deploy any obviously Marxist language. In keeping with the American political tradition, it also managed to combine hostility to the established American order with a hyper-individualist animosity to all restrictions on individuals that has been so effectively criticised by Myron Magnet.[9]

In Britain the political movements that advanced these ideas were usually egalitarian, so that the political task they set themselves was to bring about a new social order that was materially more equal. They believed their demands were legitimately one-sided because the system was unfair.

However, by the mid-1980s it was increasingly being recognised that political movements of the 1960s and 1970s that wedded political collectivism and social nihilism offered an unstable and unworkable mix. Nonetheless, a great many people of ordinary goodwill found themselves supporting some or all of these ideas because they simply wanted to help the poor. In the 1980s a counter movement developed showing that it was possible to sympathise with the least well off without being deterministic, an egocentric collectivist, an egalitarian or a cultural nihilist.

The Rediscovery of Independence

As the unexpected side-effects of the US War on Poverty became obvious, the ethos which had guided it came under strong criticism and confidence began to be restored in the earlier ideal of personal independence. Among the first critics to be taken seriously was Martin Anderson whose *Welfare* was published in 1978. George Gilder's *Wealth and Poverty* (1981) was also influential, but perhaps the main turning point was Charles Murray's *Losing Ground*, published in 1984. The essence of his argument was that, despite huge expenditures, the War on Poverty had made the conditions of the poor worse than before. Lawrence Mead soon followed with *Beyond Entitlement*. The critics attacked the four main bastions of egocentric collectivism: determinism, egalitarianism, one-sided rights, and cultural nihilism.

Equalisation

Egalitarianism was not as prominent in America as in Britain, where it came under attack because it was not compatible with either liberty or democracy. Among others, Hayek was prominent in arguing that the power of the state, and especially the law, should serve all interests and not be an instrument of class war.[10] However, there are now few defenders of equalisation and I will, therefore, focus on the more prevalent doctrines.

Determinism

In *Beyond Entitlement* Lawrence Mead strongly criticised the 'sociological determinism' of public policy makers.[11] Individual attitudes can make a difference, he argued, and to overcome 'behavioural poverty' it was important to enlist the sense of responsibility of benefit recipients. Holding people responsible was not to blame them, nor to make excuses for inaction. One-sided welfare rights were part of the problem and he advocated instead a sense of reciprocal obligation. To do so was not harsh, but rather to embrace individuals as part of a community that respected its members by protecting each from hardship while also expecting a positive contribution in return. Those who claimed that requiring work was too severe confused harshness with high expectations.

In 1987 the American Enterprise Institute published the report of a seminar group that included many of the leading lights in American poverty analysis from all points of the political spectrum. Chaired by Michael Novak, it included Lawrence Mead and Charles Murray.[12] Some poverty, said the report, could be understood as a simple lack of income, but a distinction should be drawn between poverty due to insufficient cash and 'behavioural' poverty. The pursuit of welfare policies based on the image of the beneficiary as a victim was not only failing to remedy poverty, but was causing it to increase.

They sought to understand the personal life strategies which had enabled some people to escape from poverty. They were, therefore, interested in people who began life in a bad environment, perhaps with a broken family, neighbourhood crime, drug-use and alcoholism, but who had triumphed over their circumstances. What is it, they asked, that enabled some who started with disadvantages to escape and how were they different from those who did not escape? Their conclusion was that the probability of remaining in poverty was low for those who followed three of the most mundane rules: (1) complete high school; (2) once an adult, get married and stay married (even if not on the first try, as they put it); and (3) stay employed, even if at a wage and under conditions below an individual's ultimate aims. These rules did not require super-human effort or ability, but were within the grasp of anyone. Consequently, they argued that for the able bodied, the focus of policy should be on getting people back to work by means of an independence plan which incorporated the lessons learned by those who had successfully risen above their humble origins.

For writers like Charles Murray and Michael Novak, people are social animals, much affected by upbringing, incentives and cultural norms, but also free moral agents capable of rising above their circumstances. Their emphasis on escaping from poverty by hard work and moral probity resonates powerfully with Americans, most of whom can recall the waves of poor immigrants who arrived in the USA keen to make the most of the opportunities it offered.

So far, I have been criticising 'determinism', but the issue at stake is not just the extent to which circumstances are under the control of any single individual. No less important is how individuals should orient themselves however bad the hand they have been dealt. Adam-Smith liberalism argues against determinism, without denying the obvious fact that circumstances are not under our immediate control. It also argues against fatalism and in favour of adopting a positive attitude by seeking to overcome adversity and make the most of any given situation. Egocentric collectivists, on the other hand, do not defend fatalism *per se*, but rather the futility of personal activism in the face of 'the system'. They urge instead, mass political action.

The Rights Culture

Many of the champions of self-sufficiency advocated 'workfare'— compulsory work as a condition of benefit. In response, their critics demanded to know how they could claim to be in favour of freedom when they advocated compulsion. However, the obligation to work, advocated by Mead and others, only applied to people claiming benefit at the expense of other members of the community. It was obviously open to any individual to refrain from paid work if he or she were self-supporting and demanded no benefit. The obligation of benefit recipients to work arose from their 'contract' with society. Under this two-sided agreement, the community provided a safety net which was always there, and each individual's part of the bargain was that he or she must work, if capable. To see this obligation as incompatible with liberty arises from theories of isolated individualism that have influenced collectivists and some liberals, especially from the 1960s onwards. According to these theories, the ultimate objective of a free society is 'no compulsion'. Such doctrines, however, refuse to recognise the self-contradiction in demanding to be free of the obligation to work (because there should be 'no compulsion'), when the very demand of one individual to live on benefit (and thus to be free from compulsory work) necessarily entails that others be compelled to work and pay taxes to keep him.

Writers like Mead and Novak hoped to re-create a two-sided ideal of self-reliance and community. Inspired by American history, they pictured settlers working for themselves and their families but all turning out to help both family and neighbours to clear forests and build barns, schools and churches. Each was self-reliant but also a contributor to the common welfare. This ethos of personal responsibility, combined with a personal sense of obligation to make a positive contribution to the wider community was, they believed, essential to a fulfilled life.

Thus, they urged a new conception of self-reliance and community in place of the one-sided doctrine of rights. Instead of seeing people as the bearers of rights or claims on the public purse, they saw them as contributors to the common welfare. In this view, people who failed to support themselves were also failing to be of service to others.

Cultural Nihilism and Civil Society

Novak and other neo-conservatives also attacked the cultural nihilism which had belittled tried-and-tested methods of self-improvement. Traditionally, institutions such as churches, voluntary institutions and the family taught values like personal responsibility, hard work, duty and integrity. In the 1960s and 1970s, however, self-control and the restraint of impulse were debunked.

Cultural nihilism, dressed up in the language of release from restraint, and moral relativism, defended as if it were the only alternative to authoritarianism, challenged market liberals to think about the moral framework of a free society. Francis Fukuyama, who became famous for his apparently triumphalist celebration of capitalism in *The End of History and the Last Man*,[13] summed up the changing mood. When communism collapsed in 1989 capitalism had won, but specifically, he asked, which ideas had been victorious? Was it the free-market economy alone or what might be called 'the culture of liberty'? In his later book, *Trust*, Fukuyama asked why some countries prospered when others did not—the question Adam Smith had also asked. He argues in *Trust* that the tendency was to explain success or failure as the outcome of free-market or state-interventionist policies. Few, he said, had taken seriously the possibility that 'culture' was the cause:

> Today, having abandoned the promise of social engineering, virtually all serious observers understand that liberal political and economic institutions depend on a healthy and dynamic civil society for their vitality. 'Civil Society' —a complex welter of intermediate institutions, including businesses, voluntary associations, educational institutions, clubs, unions, media, charities, churches— builds, in turn, on the family, the primary instrument by which people are socialised into their culture and given the skills that allow them to live in broader society and through which the values and knowledge of that society are transmitted across the generations.[14]

Law, contract, and economic rationality, said Fukuyama:

> provide a necessary but not sufficient basis for both the stability and prosperity of post-industrial societies; they must as well be leavened with reciprocity, moral obligation, duty towards community, and trust, which are based in habit rather than rational calculation. The latter are not anachronisms in a modern society but rather the *sine qua non* of the latter's success.[15]

Other scholars have used the term 'social capital' to describe the ability to work together for common purposes, an adaptation of the idea of 'human capital' which emphasises the importance of knowledge and skill compared with 'physical capital'.[16]

But whether we speak of the culture or of social capital, their importance was highlighted by the experience of Russia's transition from communism to capitalism. The first wave of economic advisers from the West advocated de-regulation pure and simple, but it quickly became obvious that 'getting the government out of the way' was not enough without the presence of the established habits that go hand in hand with a market economy.

The choice was not between, on the one hand, an authoritarian society in which orders must be obeyed, and on the other, the anarchy of release from all restraints and inhibitions. Adam-Smith liberals had not celebrated a social order based on obedience to authority, but nor had they sought to jettison all moral precepts. They understood that law and punishment were necessary but that the law should be kept within proper *limits*. They also knew that a society needed a moral framework—a shared sense of right and wrong—but recognised that it should not be too pervasive. This shared morality was to be upheld, not by imposition, but by the freely given support of individuals working together in the organisations that make up civil society. There would be diversity and toleration for diversity; rules and exceptions to the rule; as well as frowns of disapproval and turning a blind eye. The morality of a free society was not 'morality as the crow flies' with spies and ayatollahs seeking to punish every minor infringement. It would be a guide to living which, at any one time, offered a yardstick against which individuals could judge themselves and be judged. But the yardstick itself could change over time as yesterday's outrageous flouting of convention became today's accepted practice; or as departures from the norm once deemed harmless proved, after all, to be damaging and wrong.

The alternative offered by Adam-Smith liberals to the old authoritarian and hierarchical order was not release from all restraint, but rather participation as a moral agent in inventing, maintaining, encouraging, fostering, moulding, shaping, rejecting or renewing the common cultural property of the people. The rank and file were no longer to doff their caps to their 'betters' but instead to take part in the daily, regular routine of judging, tolerating, chiding, warning, enjoining, apologising, repenting, forgiving, being forgiven, and turning over a new leaf that is unavoidably part of the membership of any community worthy of the name. Each person was important in shaping the culture in which all shared, and with this importance came the burden of responsibility. It was not 'authoritarian' for a society to uphold an ideal way of living for its members to emulate. Indeed, a society is just such a set of ideals.

The necessity to respond to cultural nihilists, who had used some of the language of freedom, sharpened the dispute between libertarians and classical liberals. Libertarians are inclined to argue that 'values' are an inherent part of the market system, whereas classical liberals are more likely to contend that they have to be separately taught and upheld. In the libertarian view, honesty and integrity in trading relationships, for example, arise because they are mutually beneficial. They are useful and consequently widely supported. Classical liberals, however, point to the fact that some cultures stick to traditions when they serve no obviously useful purpose and have no demonstrable function. In such cases, values are upheld due to the weight of tradition and not on utilitarian grounds. One counter argument is that tradition is itself useful because it saves time. Becker, for instance, clings to the theory of man as a rational utility maximiser by arguing that adherence to tradition economises on time because reliance on established conventions eliminates the necessity to think about the rights and wrongs of every situation or action. This functional explanation, however, is equally unconvincing because many traditions do not economise on time. Often traditional practices waste time and deter economic development. As Sowell argues, we can identify 'negative human capital'.[17] Thus, values cannot be understood purely by describing the 'purpose' they serve, nor by identifying the 'function' they fulfil. They are just there, although they may also serve a purpose and have a function.

No discussion of the importance of culture could neglect the family. To be part of a community is to be born into a web of established institutions, of which the family is the most fundamental. But the husband/wife family based on marriage was among the main targets of the nihilists, chiefly because they argued that the way in which people choose to conduct their personal lives is a matter for them alone. We should not 'impose our values on others'.

Among the new champions of independence, Murray has been especially vigorous in his criticism of the manner in which public policies—particularly cash benefits for unmarried mothers—have encouraged the breakdown of the family. Other critics have called for more positive measures favouring the husband/wife family, especially recognition under the tax regime. As a result, a further dispute opened up between libertarians and classical liberals. Should the state be neutral towards the family or give encouragement to it? Libertarians object to favourable treatment of the husband/wife family on the assumption that someone who supports a free society should not advocate government measures based on a preference for any one 'lifestyle' compared with another.

There are undoubtedly aspects of private lifestyles which should be beyond the law. Such lifestyles would normally be subject to private comment and criticism, but in a liberal society there are also types of private activity which do not harm anyone else which should be free even from private criticism. But is the decision to create new human life, and then to take no responsibility at all (or little responsibility) for the child's upbringing, properly described as a lifestyle choice which should be, not only immune from criticism, but also outside the legitimate scope of the law?

First, what is the current legal position? It is that parents must financially support their own children and if one parent (usually the father) is absent he continues to be legally obliged to support the child. All civilised countries have a similar law and have always done so. Moreover, few openly argue against the present law, presumably because it is accepted that the law can properly protect a helpless infant from the selfishness of his or her parents. Consequently, the problem we face today is not so much a dispute about what the law should be, but the fact that the benefit system does not reinforce the legal position.

Despite their clear legal obligation, absent fathers are well aware that the state will, in practice, relieve them of the financial burden of keeping their children. There is a widespread feeling that it is possible to 'get away with it'. This outcome was not the explicit intention of public policy but it was the result of piecemeal measures introduced, especially since the 1970s, in the hope of making it easier for lone parents to function without the support of their absent partner. These changes, initially made on pragmatic grounds, had the effect of signalling moral approval of lone parenthood, which then had further behavioural effects leading to still more family breakdown. Thus, the benefit system made fatherless families economically more viable and socially more acceptable. It was not the only factor at work. Changes of attitude were occurring independently of the benefit system, but benefits had an independent causal effect. The net result has been that the powers of the state have been used to undermine the husband/wife family leading to increased adoption of a method of raising children which is neither economically nor socially viable.

The further outcome has been that a substantial body of public opinion does not, in practice, want to see the law enforced. Divorced men, especially those with second families, campaigned successfully against the Child Support Agency after its introduction in 1993. They paid lip service to their obligations but hoped to escape in practice. I will return to this problem below.

So far, I have discussed lone parenthood as if it were a moral issue, despite the modern reluctance to debate the issue in moral terms. Many people, however, feel more comfortable if the issue is debated on more pragmatic grounds. Which family structures work and which do not? But even if we confine our attention to 'what works', the evidence is clear and decisive.

Economically few lone parents are self-sufficient, but worse still, socially and educationally lone parenthood is not the best way of raising children. Even taking only extreme measures of the impact on the children, such as crime and drug taking, the results have been harmful. After ten years of study, one of the most authoritative commentators, Sarah McLanahan, concluded:

> Children who grow up in a household with only one biological parent are worse off, on average, than children who grow up in a household with both of their biological parents, regardless of the parents' race or educational background, regardless of whether the parents are married when the child is born, and regardless of whether the resident parent remarries. Compared with teenagers of similar background who grow up with both parents at home, adolescents who have lived apart from one of their parents during some period of childhood are twice as likely to drop out of high school, twice as likely to have a child before age twenty, and one and a half times as likely to be 'idle'—out of school and out of work—in their late teens and early twenties.[18]

These measures of the disadvantage are serious enough, but they do not take into account the countless other consequences of a missing parent. For a child to have two conscientious adults devoted to his or her well-being is a big advantage, whether the child needs help with homework, emotional support or practical advice.

Moreover, in addition to the costs for the children, there is a legitimate public interest in the outcome of child-rearing practices. The family is the primary institution for passing on the culture of a society from generation to generation. If there is an increase in the number of dysfunctional families it is harmful, not only for the children immediately affected, but also for everyone else.

To return to the original question, we can now see that to speak of a man who fathers a child and refuses to take responsibility as if he were a person exercising a 'lifestyle choice', no more and no less, neglects the fundamental issues at stake. The protection of children is a proper matter for law and, since the long-term commitment of both biological parents to their own children is highly beneficial, marriage too is properly a matter for law.

If the obligations of parents are a proper matter for law, they are also a legitimate matter for criticism. Nonetheless, there continues to be widespread animosity towards 'moralising'. On closer inspection critics of 'moralising' confine their prohibition to relatively few issues connected with sex and the institutions related to it, such as the family. They are no slower than anyone else to venture moral, ethical or prudential judgements about human conduct in other respects—including aspects of personal lifestyle, such as smoking in public places, wearing condoms during sexual encounters with strangers, or public policy towards the poor or towards foreign countries (an ethical foreign policy). Modern hostility to moralising is a hangover from the cultural nihilism of the 1970s which celebrated 'isolated individualism' and failed to see that to be part of a community is to share in its value system. To share in a value system means being guided by those values. It also means shaping their future development, either by acts of support or defiance. A society deserving of the name always and inevitably rests on a moral framework and to demand 'no moralising' is, in practice, to demand 'no community'.

As already acknowledged, there is a slight excuse for this uneasiness about moralising. A liberal society should not enforce a suffocating private morality and should tolerate a private domain free from prying eyes. But the raising of children, and particularly the decision by one parent to neglect his children, is not a purely private matter. It always has been, and should remain, the proper subject of both the law and public criticism. That this needs to be said suggests that communitarian critics like MacIntyre were right to argue that we have lost full use of the language in which past generations conducted a respectful and tolerant moral debate.[19] One of the urgent tasks of our time is to repair the damage caused by 1970s nihilism and to recover the use of this shared vocabulary.

However, this still leaves open a further question. There are three broad approaches the state could take towards the family: it could be neutral, supportive or hostile. At present, public policies tend to undermine the husband/wife family. But should the state be neutral or should it foster the family? Here there is much room for disagreement and I will venture to suggest some reforms in Chapter 4.

Public Policy Impact

Several American states have introduced reforms guided by the thinking of writers such as Mead, Murray or Novak. Three main reform strategies are now being advocated:

1. *The restoration of functions to civil society*
Advocates of this view argue that the introduction of the welfare state historically crowded out charitable and mutual alternatives which, with the benefit of subsequent experience, we can now see had many strengths compared with collectivised systems.[20]

2. *Making work pay*
This view assumes the continuance of a dominant role for the state, combined with the introduction of reforms to increase material incentives to work. The chief argument for this approach is that individuals should be better off in work than out and that additional hours of work should produce additional income. Under many systems individuals can be better off out of work or at least

only marginally better off as a result of working. The OECD is a strong advocate of this approach[21] and, as we have seen, it dominates the thinking of the present Government.

3. *Reciprocal obligation*

The third approach calls for state welfare systems to be reformed by introducing 'reciprocal obligations'. This aim can be accomplished by attaching conditions to benefits and many such schemes also provide personalised help to unemployed individuals. In particular, US workfare schemes typically require work as a condition of benefit. The latter might be called a human-capital approach because it tries to improve personal qualities, whether in the form of workplace or social skills. In the US, such policies are being openly called 'paternalistic'.[22]

The categories are not mutually exclusive. Supporters of increasing the incentives for work usually accept that those who can work should do so, but stop short of making paid employment compulsory. Advocates of the renewal of civil society and reciprocal obligation may share a common preference for increasing the role of private, voluntary or mutual organisations. Some advocates of reciprocal obligation want the state to maintain the dominant role but there are others who want informal, voluntary and commercial organisations to predominate. The issue for the latter is: to what extent can the state maintain a safety net without crowding out private effort?

Many schemes to reform welfare in America have bi-partisan support. Criticism of 1960s-style welfare put American collectivists on the defensive and led to a substantial change of heart by many. David Ellwood, Professor of Public Policy at Harvard, was typical. He has described how, in the mid 1980s, he was called upon to defend welfare. But, he says:

> the message didn't sell very well. People hated welfare no matter what the evidence. It wasn't just conservatives; liberals also expressed deep mistrust of the system, and the recipients themselves despised it.[23]

Frankly, he said, 'I had to admit that even I, who had been asked to come to the system's defence, found much to dislike'. He concluded that welfare caused conflict because it treated symptoms not causes.[24] There were three conundrums. First, the security-work conundrum meant that: 'When you give people money, food, or housing, you reduce the pressure on them to work and care for themselves'. No one, he said, 'seriously disputes this proposition'.[25] Second, there was the assistance-family structure conundrum: 'the economic insecurity of single-parent families leads to a natural desire to provide some level of support through welfare, yet such aid creates a potential incentive for the formation and perpetuation of single-parent families'.[26] Third, there was the targeting-isolation conundrum: 'Targeting tends to isolate the needy from the rest of society'.[27]

He concluded that 'the closer we move to time-unlimited, cashlike, income-tested assistance' the more we turn away from fundamental values and ignore the causes of poverty. We should focus on the expectations that a society can reasonably have of its citizens and avoid retreat into a 'neutral' world of income guarantees. Poverty, he said: 'is never simply a matter of limited income. Poverty is the result of other problems'.[28]

The American ideal, he said, was, 'not of a guaranteed income, but of a guarantee that people who strive and meet reasonable social responsibilities will be able to achieve at least a modest level of dignity and security'.[29] He attempts to define reasonable expectations for absent and custodial parents in broken families and for two-parent families. An absent parent can reasonably be expected to support his child.[30]

For custodial parents the underlying problem was that one parent was trying to do the job of two.[31] The aim of policy should be to guarantee not a minimum income, but the opportunity to achieve 'real security and independence' for mothers who were willing to work part-time.[32]

For two-parent families, it was reasonable to expect that the earnings of one person working for a full year, full-time (or the equivalent if the wife works) ought not to fall below the poverty line. He defines full-time work as 35 hours a week for 50 weeks a year, a total of 1,750 hours a year.[33]

The thinking of Ellwood and others has had a significant impact on public policy, leading to reform in many localities. Wisconsin has probably been the most successful of the American states and Chapter 4 describes the Wisconsin scheme and suggests how a similar programme could be implemented in Britain. The approach recommended in the final chapter is, wherever possible, to restore functions to civil society and, where the Government needs to be directly involved, to base policy on reciprocal obligation rather than making work pay.

4

Poverty, Work and Public Policy

Annual income £20, annual expenditure £19 19s 6d, result happiness.
Annual income £20, annual expenditure £20 0s 6d, result misery.

WHEN Dickens put these words into the mouth of Mr Micaw-
ber in *David Copperfield* he reminded us of the obvious but
easily forgotten truth that, whether people are poor or not,
depends on their expenditure as much as their income and that
some expenditure is discretionary. As Chapter 1 showed, it has
become common to treat individuals as if they were the victims of
circumstance and the policies of the Blair Government continue to
reflect this view. But just how much responsibility can individuals
be expected to assume and at what point and in what manner
should the community step in? The first step in devising a new
welfare system is to define what we can reasonably expect of each
other.

People who wish to be free and responsible members of a
community require a lifetime plan of action to allow them to be
self-sufficient and thus able to make a positive contribution to the
wealth and well-being of the society. People who have decided to
take command of their own affairs would reasonably expect to
make provision for the normal expenses of living, and for periods
when expenditure will be high—most notably when children come
along—or when income is lower, especially during retirement.
Provision also needs to be made against misfortunes such as the
early death of a partner, or illness, which may both reduce income
and increase expenditure.

If a person plans to have children, then the lifetime plan will
need to include a partner to allow for the children to be both cared
for and supported financially. Theories which assume that people
are largely, or to a significant extent, victims of circumstance, or
at the mercy of 'barriers', tend to take 'income' as a given fact not

under the control of the individual and to accept that a household is poor if income does not match expenses. However, it may be useful to state the obvious: that at any one stage of life, whether people have enough to live on will depend on four main considerations: their income; their expenditure; their earlier decisions about how best to organise their household; and their earlier provision against contingencies and lifecycle events.

Policy makers often speak of 'low pay' as if it were something entirely outside the influence of individuals. It is true that income is partly dependent on competition in the labour market, but we are not powerless. The rate of pay depends in part on skills acquired and willingness to move jobs or to change locality in order to command a higher wage. And the number of hours worked can be increased either through overtime or a second job, or another household member taking a job. The vast majority of people who escape poverty do so because they work hard and use their freedom to make the most of the conditions they find themselves in. One of the chief defects of many welfare benefits is that paying them can reduce work effort, a tendency to which family credit and working families tax credit are especially prone.

A certain amount of household expenditure is inevitable for simple survival, but some is discretionary, as earlier researchers like Rowntree recognised. The squalid conditions in which some people live are often the result of unwise expenditure. According to deterministic theories, however, to say as much is to 'blame the victim'. Household structure may also be the cause of low income and it, too, may be outside individual control, for example, when a partner is widowed or deserted. But often lone parenthood is a choice made by one or both parents, without proper consideration of the consequences for the children. Finally, we have become accustomed to relying on the state to provide against contingencies such as the death of the breadwinner or disability, and for lifecycle events such as the reduction of income during old age. However, income during retirement above the basic state pension has long been a personal responsibility with significant consequences for the standard of living.

With due allowance for factors beyond individual control, is it reasonable to expect individuals to take personal responsibility for improving their income, controlling their expenses, selecting an economically and socially viable family structure, and providing against both misfortunes and lifecycle events?

The welfare state was built on the assumption that it was not reasonable to expect anything like that degree of personal responsibility. Indeed it was built on very low, paternalistic, expectations and, step by step, it took responsibility for decisions that would have been better left to individuals. Provision against sick pay, the cost of primary medical care, and unemployment (for some) ceased to be voluntary in 1911. From 1920 most people had unemployment 'insurance', which was not insurance in the strict sense. Pensions followed under the 1925 Act.

During the 1920s and 30s it became possible to be better off out of work than in, though the impact was mitigated by the wage stop, which was introduced by the Unemployment Assistance Board in 1934 and not abolished until 1975.

From 1948 large families were subsidised, when people who could only afford a couple of children would have been better served by limiting their family. Personal responsibility for housing expenditure was diminished, at first by subsidising council rents and later by paying cash benefits. In 1967 a national scheme of rate rebates was introduced followed by a national scheme of rent rebates and allowances in 1972. In 1983 rent rebates and allowances became housing benefit.

In the 1940s and 1950s it was taken for granted that most men would work, and that couples who planned to raise children would get married in order to be self-sufficient as a family unit. However, it became possible during the 1970s to have a child outside marriage and to have enough to live on. Planning ahead in the sense of marrying a partner suitable to be a good father or mother and saving (the bottom drawer) became less important.

Thus, for a very long time public policy has been based on very low expectations of human resourcefulness. Is it realistic, therefore, to create a new welfare system based on personal responsibility? Are there any lessons to be learnt from overseas?

Wisconsin

There have been a number of successful experiments in America, of which Wisconsin is the most successful. This is how Jean

Rogers, the chief administrator in Wisconsin, summarises the objectives pursued in Wisconsin since 1987.[1]

The main thrust has been to insist on work. Education and training have not been considered adequate substitutes. However, to ensure that an early return to work was a realistic possibility, Wisconsin has found it necessary to create short-term subsidised jobs in the private and public sectors and to make available unpaid community work.

The latest development in Wisconsin is Wisconsin Works or W-2 which began in September 1997. It implements the 1996 Clinton reform which replaced Aid to Families with Dependent Children (AFDC) with Temporary Assistance for Needy Families (TANF). Six main principles can be identified:

1. Everyone who can work should work.

2. People not capable of total self-sufficiency should work within their abilities.

3. All policies should be judged by how well they strengthen the responsibility of both parents to care for their children.

4. The government should not fund behaviour it does not want more of, particularly out-of-wedlock births.

5. Benefits should not be an unconditional entitlement. They should reinforce behaviour that leads to independence and self-sufficiency.

6. Public policies should encourage communities, whether in the form of associations or local neighbourhoods, to support individual efforts to achieve self-sufficiency.[2]

Individuals seeking assistance under W-2 are offered four work options. The options are not equal. The first is the primary objective and subsequent options are offered in order of priority only as temporary expedients on the way to unsubsidised work.

1. The first priority is unsubsidised employment. To encourage the take-up of unsubsidised work, Wisconsin provides job placement help and advice about in-work benefits.

2. As a second best, subsidised employment (trial jobs) are provided. Employers can receive up to $300 a month to offset

the cost of initial training and supervision when hiring a person for 3-6 month jobs that may become permanent. (Individuals earn at least the minimum wage.)

3. When paid jobs are not possible, community service jobs are offered to those who need to learn work habits. They receive up to $555 per month and must work 30 hours a week plus ten hours training. The grant is cut if the hours are not put in.

4. The fourth option is W-2 Transition, a programme for people legitimately unable to perform self-sustaining work, either through illness, incapacity or possibly support of a relative also in W-2. They receive $518 per month and must work 28 hours per week in a community rehabilitation programme or a volunteer activity. They may also be required to spend 12 hours in training. They are also subject to substance abuse evaluation and counselling, where applicable.

No less important than encouraging self-sufficiency through work is the encouragement of intact families. Here the government has to be content with indirect methods, for merely by passing laws it cannot bring about a restoration of the husband/wife family as the normal method of raising children. It can, however, avoid policies that make matters worse.

In Wisconsin, teenage parents are required to finish school and live at home or in supervised hostels. There are no cash entitlements for unmarried teenage mothers and no cash benefits for any parent without the work obligation, unless their child is under 12 weeks of age.[3] Custodial parents are required to co-operate in identifying the non-custodial parent as a condition of participation in W-2. In return, full child support payments go to custodial parents and not to the welfare agency.

The obligation of fathers to support their children is rigorously enforced. All non-custodial parents are required by law to become more employable so that they can support their children. Failure to participate in work experience or training can lead to jail. In certain cases where paid work is not an immediate possibility, they may be allowed to meet their obligation by taking part in unpaid work or training for 16 weeks. Many try to avoid payment, arguing that they are not able to contribute. However, when confronted with the three stark choices—pay child support, spend 16 weeks in unpaid community work experience, or go to jail—75 per cent find that they can pay after all. This is called the 'smoke-out effect'.[4]

The Wisconsin style of workfare has been criticised because work is compulsory, as if there were an option that could involve no compulsion at all. The difficulty is that when an individual refuses to work because he is better off on benefits he is taking it for granted that other people will be compelled by the government to give some of their income to him. The only consistent stance for the person who wishes to avoid all compulsion is to call for no money to be given whatsoever. But if cash assistance is to be made available, then the real issue is how to give it without doing more harm than good. Wisconsin's approach might be called 'positive paternalism' because its intention is to restore independence. And it can be contrasted with 'negative paternalism', the attitude of those who are content to pay benefits, whether out of sympathy or a pragmatic desire to keep the poor quiet. Social security systems which require work, or offer a personalised employment service, do so in order to restore people to independence. If they are paternalistic, then they are only open to that complaint in the short term. The sole justification for their temporary resort to paternalism is the restoration of independence. As Chapter 3 argued, the relationship between claimants and the state may also be viewed as a contract. The contract between the state and individuals requires the state to maintain a national minimum and individuals to work if they are able. Since the presence of a legal obligation to support individuals who are out of work creates a temptation to take advantage of the taxpayer's generosity, it is legitimate to enforce the contract on both parties.

Could such a scheme be implemented in Britain? Is it too harsh?

Proposals for Reform

My earlier books, *Reinventing Civil Society* and *Community Without Politics*, advocated a bigger role for charity and mutual aid associations in the provision of welfare services and I will not repeat those arguments here. In any event, such measures will take time to implement and the purpose of the present chapter is to make the case for more immediate reforms that could help to reduce welfare dependency in the short run.

Two main proposals are made. First, that we urgently need to redefine the social contract between the community and its members. The safety net should always be there to prevent hardship, but we need to reconsider what the members of a society can reasonably expect of benefit claimants. This essay suggests a different method of combining an ever-present safety net with a stronger focus on self-sufficiency.

Second, we should abolish all entitlements to benefit and, instead, place a two-part obligation on the Government: to provide assistance sufficient to prevent severe hardship to all who ask; and to do so in a manner most likely to lead to self-sufficiency.

First, some general remarks about national insurance and 'entitlements' are necessary. Among those who accept the necessity for radical welfare reform are people who want to restore the national insurance basis of the social security system.[5] They believe it will avoid the necessity for a discretionary system of social assistance.

During the course of the century it came to be accepted that people who needed help should be given it as of right and not as an act of kindness. Charity came to be associated with stigma and subservience. This distinction between 'benefits as an entitlement' and 'charitable assistance at the discretion of the donor' has its roots in the private welfare systems that pre-dated the welfare state. Before the watershed legislation, the 1911 National Insurance Act, it was common to make a distinction between charity and mutual aid. Those who had contributed to a friendly society thought of their benefits as a right, earned by their earlier contributions, and they prided themselves on never asking for charity. The 1911 scheme built on this distinction by extending the friendly society benefits to everyone by compulsion.

Before 1911 friendly society members could genuinely claim to be entitled to their benefits, which were paid from a common fund accumulated from the small but regular contributions of members. However, from the very beginning national insurance had a 'something for nothing' element ('ninepence for fourpence', as Lloyd George put it while recommending the legislation to the

House of Commons). The full cost was not met by the members. Moreover, by 1920 payments were being made to unemployed workers without regard to their contributions and the payments were treated as an entitlement justified by earlier sacrifices, when they were no such thing.

Campaigners for national insurance have typically wanted to reduce the need for discretion. However, the poor law continued to offer discretionary benefits until 1948, only to be replaced by a similar discretionary system, national assistance.

Neither the poor law nor national assistance were benefits awarded as of right. We have become accustomed to speaking of benefits as a right but, until 1966, individuals had no legal right to non-contributory benefits. Instead, the public authorities had a *duty* to assist. This difference is more than semantic. The entitlement ethos has led to increased willingness to claim and a reduced sense of personal obligation. It has also weakened the ability of public officials to discourage claimants from reducing their work effort.

Beveridge expected national assistance would be a residual scheme for a relatively few people, but during the post-war years the number of claimants grew, and far from reducing the need for an uninsured safety net, if anything, national insurance had the effect of increasing the sense of entitlement for both contributory and non-contributory benefits. When national assistance was renamed supplementary benefit in 1966, it too became a legal entitlement, thus eradicating all but a formal distinction between insured and non-insured benefits.

In many ways we have now come full circle and find ourselves repeating mistakes made by an earlier generation. When legislators in 1911 had in mind a distinction between (mutually insured) benefits as of right and charitable assistance, they obliterated a distinction considered by many to be fundamental. During the nineteenth and early twentieth centuries a distinction was not only made between charity and mutual aid, but also between two kinds of charity: the dole charities and the visiting charities. Like governments in our own time, the dole charities associated kindness with 'refraining from judgement'. They gave cash without questions. The 'visiting' charities, however, tried to restore self-respect and independence and believed that to give cash without practical advice and encouragement to be independent was a failure of responsibility—the easy option. Governments since the 1920s have increasingly given benefits as a right and repeated the error of the old dole charities. The unavoidable reality is, however, that benefits can only be a contractual entitlement if the claimant is genuinely insured.

To try to build a future welfare system on national insurance is a distraction because most of the people today who are dependent on means-tested benefits have no national insurance entitlement and could not genuinely qualify in the near future. The challenge, therefore, is to devise a method of giving help to them that will restore genuine independence. If it is to be effective, such help must be discretionary because, apart from their reliance on benefits, claimants often have little else in common. The causes of their dependence are numerous and each requires a more personal service than the modern social security system has ever provided.

Another distraction is the contrast that is often made between 'universal benefits' and 'means testing'. The real distinction is between assistance according to category and assistance according to personal circumstances. Each person should be treated as unique and provided with the personal help needed to become as self-sufficient as possible.

The perverse effects of means-tested benefits have come under sharp criticism in recent years, but the remedy is not to resort to 'universal' benefits. Both means-tested and universal benefits involve the categorisation of individuals. The categories rarely make sense in all cases and so the system tends to devise more complex rules to accommodate diverse individual circumstances. In turn, the additional complexity tends to produce unexpected, sometimes perverse, results. The difficulties are made worse by the 'moral hazard' inherent in all insurance-based schemes (public or private) which pay claims when the formal conditions to be met are under the control of the claimant. Schemes that make payments to the workless are especially vulnerable to such moral hazard for the obvious reason that unemployment may be voluntary. The better approach is to accept the unavoidable diversity of the human condition and the moral hazard inherent in benefit schemes and to introduce a discretionary system, permitting officials to provide help that is best calculated to restore independence, with the ever-present safeguard that no one must be allowed to suffer severe hardship. Wisconsin has led the way in developing such a system, with considerable success. As Mead has argued, it is not an easy transformation and it took several years in Wisconsin to recruit suitable public servants and outside contractors, but it can be done.[6]

Thus, the purpose of a discretionary welfare system should be to avoid pigeon-holing people and to take into account each individual's full circumstances with the intention of helping them to become as self-sufficient as possible. In most cases, complete self-support through work should be the aim, but for some, only partial self-sufficiency will be attainable.

The distinction between contributory and non-contributory benefits should be abolished and a single income-replacement benefit introduced. It should be given a name such as 'transitional assistance' to emphasise that it is providing temporary support to help people back on their feet.

Reasonable Obligations

Each family can reasonably be expected to accept three obligations: to work enough hours to meet normal living expenses; to provide against misfortunes which prevent self-support, such as illness; and to provide for predictable lifecycle events, such as the cost of raising children and the fall in income that may accompany retirement from work as age takes its toll.

The Obligation To Work

What should the work obligation mean in practice? This study sets out to define 'reasonable obligations' for three main groups: the able bodied, single parents, and disabled people.

Reasonable Work Obligations: Able-Bodied People

I take it for granted that the state should maintain a safety net and in doing so it should attach conditions to encourage an early return to work by able-bodied people. New applicants should be subject to strict requirements before any benefit is paid. All new applicants should meet a personal adviser to determine their capacity for self-sufficiency. It is reasonable to expect people to have sufficient savings to cover two weeks without income and so anyone wanting cash assistance should be required to take part in two weeks of job search before benefit is payable. Any emergency cash assistance required during that time should be treated as a repayable loan. Where one parent is absent, the payment of child support should be investigated immediately. Once in receipt of a benefit the main aim should be to direct the claimant towards work in the manner of Wisconsin.

The introduction of jobseeker's allowance (JSA) in place of unemployment benefit was a substantial move in the right direction. Recipients of JSA are expected to be making a genuine effort to find full-time work. However, they are not ultimately *required* to find work, whereas in Wisconsin an employment adviser would in effect tell the claimant: 'Here is a job. Here is the address. Report at 9.00 in the morning or your benefit will be stopped.' The Blair Government intends to require claimants to attend an interview, but it will be perfectly legitimate for them to turn up and announce that they have no intention of working.

The Wisconsin approach is highly directive, but it recognises that some people have a genuine difficulty in finding and keeping work and the system provides safeguards for them while ensuring that the able-bodied idler has to find a job. As in Wisconsin, a graded series of alternatives should also be provided for people not yet ready for full-time work. But unsubsidised work should always be the first choice with other options only temporary until the ultimate objective of unsubsidised paid employment is met.

Training should not be ranked as an equal alternative to work. Unfortunately Labour's original new deal for the 18-24 age-group treated training as one of four equal options, but it can too easily be used as a tactic to delay finding a job and the first priority should be to obtain paid work. In any event, work and training are not mutually exclusive alternatives. All work involves learning of some kind, formal or informal. It is sometimes said that people will be pushed into 'dead-end jobs', but there is no such thing as a dead-end job, only the first rung on the ladder. As in Wisconsin, any financial assistance for training should be given in the form of repayable loans or partial grants. Trainees should always pay a substantial part of the cost to ensure that they are fully committed to training as part of their career plan and not as a tactic to delay a return to self-sufficiency.

In Wisconsin, in order to make the work obligation a reality at all stages of the economic cycle it was found necessary to create subsidised private or public-sector jobs and to set up community work schemes. Such arrangements have already been made under the new deal and could easily be extended. However, the subsidy should not be conditional upon the provision of training but seen rather as a device for creating jobs to which individuals can be directed for short periods. At the same time, if training or rehabilitation are provided, so much the better.

Directive measures are usually attacked as harsh, but not so long ago more stringent measures were applied in Britain. The Blair Government's approach to the possibility that a person could receive more in benefits while out of work than from working, has been to increase in-work benefits to 'make work pay'. As we have seen, such measures have behavioural consequences.

Until 1975 the 'wage stop' was used as an alternative. Both the 1948 National Assistance Act and Labour's 1966 Ministry of Social Security Act provided for a wage stop, that is, the amount of assistance was not normally to exceed the income a person could receive if he were in full-time employment. The rule applied to unemployed persons and recipients of sick pay (during the first six months of their claim). A Ministry report of 1967 found about 15,000 families on assistance who were wage-stopped.[7] The wage stop was cancelled in 1975 when about 6,000 unemployed persons were affected by it. The maximum number affected had been 35,000 in 1970, but in the view of the Supplementary Benefits Commission (SBC), the need had been reduced by the introduction of in-work benefits including rent rebates and allowances, rate rebates and family income supplement.[8] The SBC's 1975 annual report captured the mood—at its height in the mid-1970s—of those who attributed no responsibility at all to the individual:

The Commission recognises that the abolition of the wage stop has given rise to some public disquiet about reports of men whose benefit levels appear to be disproportionately high when compared with the general level of wages. There are, however, very few such cases and they arise only where a man has a larger than average family to support, pays a high rent and has poor prospects of obtaining well-paid work.

In such cases, said the Commission:

> there may be little incentive to find work, even taking into account the family income supplement and housing allowances to which he would probably be entitled. The real solution seems to lie not in reducing benefit to these families but in a generous level of family support, a raising of tax thresholds for low wage-earners and higher levels of earnings.[9]

The advantage of the wage stop was that it encouraged self-improvement and personal responsibility. It gave individuals a reason not to have children they could not afford and encouraged them to increase their earning capacity where possible. To pay benefits regardless of work effort has encouraged more childbirths and discouraged the acquisition of skills which would enhance wages.

Under the 1948 Act the National Assistance Board could also refuse assistance to individuals who were unemployed without good reason and who refused offers of jobs. However, in practice the sanction could not be used against married men because they were inclined to live off the assistance given to their families. For such cases the 1948 Act provided two further sanctions: first, they could be sent to a re-establishment centre for retraining in the habits of work; or, they could be prosecuted for failing to maintain themselves and their families through work.

In 1966 there were two residential and six non-residential re-establishment centres whose aim was 'not to teach a man a trade but simply to reintroduce him to the habits, routine and demands of a normal working life'.[10] In 1975 there were 15 re-establishment centres, including three residential, which catered for about 2,000 men. The philosophy was similar. They were designed to 'revive the will to work, to restore the habit of getting up and going to work and to give men confidence in their ability to hold down a job under normal circumstances'.[11] In 1979 there were 17 centres which catered for about 2,200 men.[12] Three were exclusively re-establishment centres and the remainder were also reception centres for people 'without a settled way of living' (known as resettlement units after the 1980 Act).[13] In the late 1970s, a man who 'refuses or neglects to maintain himself' could be required to attend a re-establishment centre as a condition of continued receipt of benefit.[14] Under Section 10 of the Supplementary Benefits Act, the procedure was to report such men to the Supplementary Benefits Appeal Tribunal which decided whether or not to pay benefit only on attendance at a centre. In 1977 the tribunal sent 194 out of 202 men referred to it to centres and in 1978, 238 out of 244.[15]

However, the Government announced its intention to close the re-establishment centres (and the resettlement units) in 1985 and implemented the decision in stages. The courses provided by the re-establishment centres were supposed to be provided by the Manpower Services Commission. However, as the civil service unions pointed out at the time, the re-establishment centres had provided for individuals with social and behavioural problems whereas the Manpower Services Commission did not.[16]

The second sanction, criminal prosecution, was used sparingly. In the early 1950s about 50 men a year were prosecuted, but the number rose steadily and had reached 178 by 1965. The great majority were convicted and between half and two-thirds were jailed.[17] This power was continued under Labour's Ministry of Social Security Act, 1966, which replaced national assistance with supplementary benefit. The Act also made benefit an entitlement for the first time, but the expectation that an able-bodied person would work remained strong. Prosecutions continued but at a lower level. In 1972 criminal proceedings were taken against 17 unemployed persons for 'persistent refusal or neglect to maintain themselves, and their families where they had dependants'. Three were jailed and two given suspended prison sentences.[18] During the 1970s prosecution for failure to be self-supporting seems to have fallen out of favour, although criminal proceedings were taken against seven people in 1978 for persistent refusal or neglect to maintain themselves (and their dependants) under section 25 of the Supplementary Benefits Act.[19] Criminal proceedings continued to be pursued against 'liable relatives', that is persons who failed to support their dependants (to be discussed below).

A further sanction had been introduced in 1968 following an 'anti-scrounger' campaign in the press. It followed the practice of the Birmingham Public Assistance Committee in the 1930s, which awarded benefit to some claimants with a warning that at the end of four weeks assistance would only be available in the workhouse.[20] The main difference was that in 1968 there was no workhouse and so to stop benefits after four weeks was more harsh. Nonetheless, occasionally benefit was awarded for four weeks only when it was felt that a person was capable of work and fit for work.[21] In 1971 a further sanction was made available. Benefit recipients judged to be voluntarily unemployed could have their benefit cut by 40 per cent.[22]

During the 1980s the problem of benefit dependency continued to be a concern. The 1980 Rayner Scrutiny recommended a stricter work test but, despite changes, the system was still considered unsatisfactory in the mid-1980s. Under the 1986 Social Security Act, the period of disqualification from receipt of unemployment benefit was increased for refusing to take a suitable job, voluntary unemployment, leaving without good cause, or being sacked for misconduct. From 1986 the period of disqualification was increased from six weeks to 13 weeks, and in 1988 from 13 to 26 weeks. Also in 1986 a more rigorous questionnaire was introduced along with Restart interviews for those unemployed for one year, and in 1987 the Employment Service was established to adopt a more positive attitude to helping claimants find work. Previously benefit payment and job assistance had been largely separate enterprises and the Employment Service took over about 1,000 job centres and 1,000 unemployment benefit offices and began converting them to integrated offices.

These measures were not considered to have been sufficiently effective and the 1989 Social Security Act went further still by ending the requirement to be available for 'suitable' employment. Subsequently a person must be available for any job he could 'reasonably be expected to do' and after 13 weeks he should accept any job. The definition of 'good cause' for refusing a job was also tightened, but remained vague. From 1989 claimants were expected to demonstrate job search and to retain proof of their efforts. However, an initial study by Bryson and Jacobs found the measures not to have been very effective.[23]

Concern continued into the 1990s and earlier measures were reinforced in 1990. The Employment Service became an executive agency and in that year Back to Work Plans were also introduced. The next major changes came in October 1996 with the jobseeker's allowance which reduced the period of benefit receipt from 12 to six months and increased pressure to find work.

Thus, during the 1960s and even into the 1970s, effective sanctions to encourage an early return to work were available to the authorities and often used. They began to be weakened during the 1970s and, despite Conservative rhetoric, the weakening continued during the 1980s. Towards the end of the 1980s the Government introduced some new measures but they mainly relied on incentives and advice rather than the enforcement of the obligation to work. Throughout the Tory years, sanctions, including criminal prosecution, continued to be available but were not used to good effect. By the end of their 18 years, when the JSA was introduced, the Conservatives were moving towards a system based on reciprocal obligation, but it fell a long way short of the ideal. Labour's new deal for the 18-24s, discussed in Chapter 1, has so far come closest.

Reasonable Work Obligations: Broken Families

For recipients of jobseeker's allowance there is typically an able-bodied person out of work who needs to be steered towards a suitable workplace. However, the majority of lone parents are on income support (although they can opt to receive JSA) and face a different problem: that one (perhaps both) parents has decided to adopt a lifestyle that is incompatible with self-sufficiency. Quite apart from the emotional and educational impact on the children, it is not possible for any parent simultaneously to work and care for young children.[24] A highly-paid single parent may be able to afford to pay for childcare out of his or her wages, but the great majority cannot.

Governments can adopt one of three general attitudes to the family: neutrality; to privilege marriage; or to privilege *non-*

marriage. In recent years public policies have consistently privileged *non*-marriage and the urgent priority is to stop rewarding behaviour which has harmful effects on children.

Before turning to the recommendations, it will be useful to look at how we arrived in the current situation. A variety of measures since the 1960s and 1970s have privileged lone parenthood, sometimes by giving more cash while out of work, and in more recent years by linking benefits to the performance of part-time work.

Since 1966 long-term additions have been paid to recipients of income support or its predecessors. In 1973 two scales were introduced: the ordinary and the long-term. The long-term rate was some 25 per cent higher and was paid to pensioners immediately and all others—including lone parents—after two years, except the unemployed. From November 1980 the long-term rate was paid after only one year.[25]

From 1988 the long-term rate was abolished and replaced by premiums for particular groups. According to the green paper on social security reform of 1985, some 70 per cent of lone parents were receiving the long-term rate. It was replaced by a premium rate paid to all lone parents with children under 16 regardless of the length of time on benefit.[26] In addition to the lone parent premium and the family premium, lone parents aged 18-24 were also to receive the rate for single persons over 25.

In 1999/2000 this structure remained, although the lone parent premium for new claimants had been abolished in June 1998, having been renamed the family premium (lone parent) from April 1997. (The 1997/98 lone parent premium was £4.95.) However, those already receiving it continued to do so and the reduction was partly restored by increases in the family premium from April 1999. Lone parents continued to receive the higher than normal rate, if under 25 years of age. The normal single person's allowance in 1999/2000 for those aged 18-24 was £40.70. Lone parents received the 25+ rate of £51.40. (The rate for a couple, of whom one is over 18, was only £80.65.) In addition, lone parents received £13.90 (if new to income support) or £15.75 (if they had previously been entitled to the higher premium rate) plus additions for dependent children and housing costs.

Lone parents have also profited from higher earnings disregards. It had long been the practice to allow recipients of benefit to earn a small amount per week. In 1976 a special higher earnings disregard for lone parents was introduced[27] and subsequent earnings disregards were more generous still. In 1999/2000 lone parents receive a £15 disregard for income support, when normally it is £5 per person (£10 for a couple). In addition, a special £25 disregard for housing benefit and council tax benefit is available; and for housing benefit, council tax benefit and family credit the first £15 of any maintenance is disregarded.

The introduction of child benefit in 1977 also boosted the income of lone parents. Previously family allowance had been paid only for second and subsequent children. From April 1977 all children received child benefit up to age 16 or until 19, if in full-time education. Moreover, child benefit was paid at a higher rate for lone parents—the special one-parent benefit. From April 1997 it was renamed, child benefit (lone parent), and abolished for new cases from June 1998. Part of the reduction was restored by increasing child benefit by £2.50 from April 1999. (One-parent benefit was worth £6.05 at 1997/98 rates.)

Just as disregards and means-tested benefits have been modified to give a privileged status to lone parents, so too have the main in-work benefits: family income supplement 1971-1988, family credit 1988-1999 and subsequently working families tax credit. Reform of these benefits has been driven as much by a desire to encourage lone parents to work part-time as anything else.

By supplementing total weekly income family income supplement (FIS) gave people an incentive to reduce their hours of work, an incentive effect that has increased over the years as the minimum number of hours required to qualify for benefit has been reduced. The tendency of family credit to encourage reduced work effort was belatedly recognised in 1995 with the payment of an additional £10 (now £11.05) to family credit claimants who worked at least 30 hours per week.

The introduction of family income supplement (FIS) followed acceptance of the arguments of the poverty lobby after the 'rediscovery' of in-work poverty in the 1960s. The main alternative approach defended at the time was to increase family allowance, but the cost was felt to be prohibitive and the consequence was the introduction of a means-tested in-work benefit. Little notice was taken of the danger that it would have behavioural effects on employers and claimants, but within months the new term 'poverty trap' had been coined by Frank Field and David Piachaud.[28]

During the 1970s FIS was received by relatively few people. In 1979 only 78,000 were in receipt, but in that year the value of benefit was increased and the minimum number of hours was reduced for lone parents but not couples. In 1971 FIS defined full-time work as 30 hours per week, but from April 1979 lone parents qualified for FIS if they worked only 24 hours a week. Initially, an additional 10,000 qualified,[29] and overall the number of recipients increased from 78,000 to 204,000 between 1979 and 1983.[30]

In 1988 FIS became family credit and subsequent changes made it still more appealing to lone parents, especially after 1992. In that year, the hours of work per week required to qualify were reduced from 24 to 16. The early 1990s also saw a huge advertising campaign to encourage the take-up of family credit.

In October 1994 came the introduction of the childcare allowance for family credit claimants, permitting them to receive up to £40 of the cost of professional childcare for children under 11. The terms were such that the overwhelming majority of claimants were lone parents. In 1996 the childcare allowance was increased to a maximum of £60.

During the years when these measures were being enacted, the number of lone parents claiming benefit was rising steadily. In 1951 89,000 claimants were described as unmarried mothers, separated, divorced or deserted wives, some 6 per cent of claimants. By 1991 there were 1,056,000 one-parent families claiming income support, 18 per cent of the total.[31]

The growing number of lone parents mostly reflects actual family breakdown. However, a further consequence of rewarding lone parenthood has been to encourage fictitious family breakdown. Some couples present themselves to the authorities as two separate households in order to increase their benefits, when they actually live as man and wife. This tendency has long been recognised and successive governments have tried to discourage it, particularly by means of the 'co-habitation' rule, later called 'living together as husband and wife'. The 1994 Benefit Review found that about one-third (£450m) of income support and unemployment benefit fraud of £1.4 billion per year was due to couples falsely claiming to be living separately.[32]

The Obligations of Absent Parents: Public policies should put the interests of children first and bear in mind the easily-forgotten truth that in the vast majority of cases there are two living parents: one absent and the other custodial (or 'non-resident parents' and 'parents/persons with care' in DSS jargon).

Most custodial single parents are lone mothers and, as in Wisconsin, the first priority should be to ensure that the absent father is meeting the cost of raising his own children. In some cases, the amount that fathers can pay will allow the respective mothers to avoid work altogether, and in all cases it will enable them to be self-supporting with the addition of income from part-time work. DSS studies have found that maintenance payments increase the likelihood of income support recipients taking a job, especially inexperienced workers or the poorly educated.[33] According to Alan Marsh, if paid to lone parents in amounts sufficient to meet the cost of childcare, 'maintenance payments all but abolish their poverty trap'.[34]

Again, it is necessary to have available some sanctions against wilfully errant fathers, including jail. Such measures were taken for granted until recently. The 1948 National Assistance Act enabled the National Assistance Board (NAB) to trace and prosecute men who failed to maintain their dependants. In 1965 the board prosecuted 594 such men and 244 were sent to prison. The 1965 NAB annual report acknowledged that the process was costly but argued that it was necessary 'not only to bring home to the man his liability to maintain his dependants but also to deter other would-be offenders'.[35] A table in *Social Security Statistics 1982* gives the number of criminal prosecutions of 'liable relatives' for every year from 1967 to 1982. In 1967 there were 716 prosecutions leading to 52 jail sentences. Every year until 1982 there were about 500-600 prosecutions. In 1982 there were 356 leading to 37 prison sentences.[36] However, criminal proceedings fell out of favour in the 1980s and in 1989 there were only 39 prosecutions leading to two jail sentences. In 1991 there were four prosecutions none of which resulted in prison sentences.[37] In 1993 the Child Support Agency took over responsibility for child maintenance, although a husband and wife are still responsible for supporting each other. Criminal prosecution continues to be available to the DSS and should be used.

In Wisconsin absent parents are required to pay a percentage of their income towards the upkeep of their child. The Blair Government proposed a similar formula in its July 1998 discussion document. The payment will be 15 per cent of net income for one child, 20 per cent for two, and 25 per cent for three or more.[38] It is certainly preferable to the complex formula used by the CSA since 1993. However, one of the factors which undermined the CSA was its enforcement of the same formula on both divorced and unmarried men. In the early 1990s public opinion was strongly against unmarried men who fathered a child and refused to take any responsibility. The CSA proceeded to direct its energy disproportionately against divorced men, some of whom were subject to existing court orders, and some of whom felt they had been wronged by an adulterous wife who had been given custody of the children, when the men would have preferred to look after them.

To avoid unfairness, all maintenance cases involving marriage breakdown should be dealt with by a judicial process leading to an independent judgement made after hearing both sides.[39] One of the defects of our current divorce law is that it tends to assume that marriage breakdowns typically involve an amicable parting of the ways. But in many cases one partner selfishly walks out on the other, imposing costs on the spouse and the children. No-fault divorce enjoys considerable support, but we have not yet struck the right balance between, on the one hand, the interests of the children and, on the other, the interests of parents. An individual who breaks a hire-purchase agreement for a video player is in more legal trouble than a man who abandons a wife and her infant child. It is not immediately obvious that this is a sensible state of affairs.

In clear-cut cases of desertion, when one partner leaves both spouse and children, he or she should be required to pay the living expenses of the custodial parent, in addition to child support. Any absent parent should, in all circumstances, be expected to maintain his own children, but the additional sanction of paying the spouse's living expenses would signal strong disapproval of desertion and provide a powerful incentive for loyalty. It goes without saying that no such regime should be applied to couples who merely live together outside marriage. They cannot expect to enjoy the protection of marriage without its obligations.

The Obligations of Custodial Parents: Having required the father to pay the maximum support possible, the mothers should then be required to work to the extent necessary to avoid welfare dependency. A married mother who had been deserted would, of course, not be expected to work because the courts would require her former husband to keep her. (Naturally, a deserted husband would be subject to the same rules.) Similarly, widows and widowers with dependent children would face no work obligation. But all other custodial single parents who asked for welfare benefits would be subject to the same work requirement as other able-bodied persons. The ultimate objective would be an unsubsidised job, but in the meantime the public authorities would find them subsidised work or require their participation in a community project in return for benefit.

The chief difficulty is deciding when the work obligation for the custodial parent should be imposed. Practices vary from country to country.[40] In Sweden, lone parents are expected to work when their youngest child is aged one; in France it is three years; in Germany part-time work is required when the youngest child reaches school age and full-time work when aged 14. In Britain, there is no obligation until the youngest child is 16. Many people would argue that pre-school children are better off in the care of their mother than in childcare institutions, however well trained the staff might be. The evidence very strongly supports that view, especially for children up to the age of two or three.[41]

The chief counter argument is that public policy should be calculated to deter future out-of-wedlock births and that imposing a work obligation on the mother, plus a child-support obligation on the absent father, is the best method. In Wisconsin, for example, lone parents must work when their youngest child is 12 weeks old, because a married woman who chose to work would be expected to return at that time. Many married women do choose to work in these circumstances. Moreover, the British Government actively encourages them to do so by subsidising childcare from general taxes. In most cases the child will be worse off in a childcare institution than with his or her mother, but the mothers either do not accept that fact or believe it is counter-balanced by the advantages of working.

Because there are trade-offs to be made, many would argue that the matter should be left to personal choice and the lone-parent lobby groups use the same argument on behalf of lone mothers. However, the position of a lone parent is different from that of a married women. It is precisely because she is married that the latter is able to choose between work and childcare. In the vast majority of cases an unmarried mother could only have the same power of choice by getting married, but when the state provides cash assistance it reduces the pressure to marry (or re-marry).

Marriage not only makes it possible for mothers to choose between work and childcare, it is also overwhelmingly in the interests of children. When children are brought up by two committed parents, the children benefit substantially.[42]

An obligation to go out to work is very likely to encourage marriage. Young females who might have babies outside wedlock in the belief that the baby is a passport to independence will be deterred from doing so; and those who became pregnant anticipating that the father would support them, only to be deserted by him, will have a strong reason to find a more suitable partner at the earliest possible opportunity, an outcome which is better for both them and their child. Altogether, there are likely to be far fewer children born without both a mother and a father committed to their well being.

Deciding at what age the work obligation should apply is a real conundrum. I suspect that there is a consensus for a work obligation when the youngest child reaches school age, and such an obligation should be imposed at the earliest date. However, I believe that we should impose the work obligation at an earlier age to encourage marriage. The simplest method would be to apply the Wisconsin principle, namely that the work obligation of lone parents should be no different from that of married mothers. In Britain, statutory maternity pay lasts for 18 weeks from the date the mother stops working. For lone mothers, an obligation to work when the child was 18 weeks old would create reasonable equality.

Experience has shown that, if the government substitutes for the father, the results for the child are harmful; the mother experiences a lower income than if married; and the number of parents who opt for non-marriage increases. Consequently, an obligation to work is in the long-term interests of both mother and child because it is likely to reduce the incidence of lone parenthood.

To impose a work obligation on lone parents raises the problem of childcare costs. Wisconsin found it necessary to provide assistance with childcare costs to low-income families in the form of co-payments which never exceed 16 per cent of income.[43] Under working families tax credit, an extremely costly system of subsidised childcare is to be introduced. However, under family credit, childcare costs can be disregarded for those who earn more than the threshold above which maximum benefit starts to be reduced. This means that individuals working only a few hours do not receive childcare costs. There is economic sense in this arrangement, because there is no economic gain in giving an incentive to mothers to work for wages less than or similar to the cost of childcare. This sensible restriction has been eliminated under the working families tax credit.

More important still, mothers capable of earning little more than the cost of childcare do not need a job, they need a husband. And if the husband cannot pay enough in maintenance to keep them, public policy should not encourage them to continue their lifestyle or encourage others to adopt it.

One approach would be to require custodial parents to work for the number of hours a week necessary to lift them off benefit and for the state to pay the necessary childcare costs. However, the purpose of the work obligation is not only to create self-sufficiency but also to withdraw the privileged status of non-marriage. Childcare costs should, therefore, be met but then deducted from earnings down to the income support (transitional assistance) level so that in certain circumstances a lone parent would be working for several hours a week for the equivalent of income support. Few will want to continue and the likely result will be that more unmarried mothers and unmarried fathers will get married and that fewer children will be born outside wedlock. Such a regime would also make fictitious lone parenthood (discussed above) less financially attractive.

As Charles Murray has consistently argued, once a lone parent is on benefit, the payment should not be increased for additional children born out of wedlock. In Wisconsin births within ten months of the first benefit payment are not affected but, to encourage a responsible attitude to pregnancy, subsequent births receive no extra cash. A similar rule should be enforced in Britain.

Reasonable Work Obligations: Disabled People

What is the system now? If you have a job and become unable to work you are entitled to statutory sick pay (SSP) after four consecutive days of incapacity. It is paid by employers for up to 28 weeks at a rate of £59.55 (in 1999/2000) per week but not for the first three days of incapacity. During the 28-week period, inability to work is assessed according to the 'own occupation' test, that is, to be eligible you must be unable to carry out your usual occupation. After 28 weeks an individual who is still unable to work becomes eligible for incapacity benefit (IB)

Incapacity benefit replaced sickness benefit and invalidity benefit in April 1995. It is paid to people who are assessed as being incapable of work and who meet national insurance contribution conditions. After 28 weeks on SSP (or from the start of the claim for people who did not previously have a job) eligibility is based on the 'all work' test, which assesses ability to carry out a range of work-related activities. There are two lists of activities, one for physical disabilities and one for mental. Points are awarded for inability to perform defined tasks. For example:

Cannot walk up and down one stair   15 points

Cannot walk up and down a flight of 12 stairs
without holding on and taking a rest   7 points

To be classified incapable of work a person must score 15 points from the physical disabilities list; or ten points from the mental disabilities list; or 15 from both combined (with a minimum of six from the mental disabilities list).

The Child Poverty Action Group (CPAG), among other organisations, gives advice about how to 'pass' the test. For example, the CPAG's *Rights Guide to Non-Means-Tested Benefits*, recommends 'the tactics you should employ' at each stage. For example, the doctors employed by the Benefits Agency Medical Service (BAMS) have no special expertise, says the CPAG:

> Unless a doctor has actually observed you performing an activity, which, in most cases the BAMS doctor will not have done, there is no reason in principle why his or her view on, say, whether or not you are able to climb stairs without holding on and taking a rest should be any more valid than your own view or the view of a relative, friend or colleague who has observed you trying to perform this task on a daily basis.[44]

The guide then offers 'a few tips for completing the questionnaire'.[45] The use of terms like 'tips' and 'tactics' gives the game away.

For people under state pension age the higher short-term rate of £59.55 is paid for weeks 29 to 52 of entitlement. An adult dependant receives an additional £31.15. People not entitled to SSP receive the lower short-term rate for the first 28 weeks (£50.35.)

The long-term rate of incapacity benefit applies to people under state pension age who have been sick for more than a year (including any period on SSP). It is £66.75 plus £39.95 for adult dependants and extra amounts for children. In addition, recipients are also entitled to income support, housing benefit and council tax benefit.

There were 1,644,640 recipients of IB in May 1998.[46] The growth in the number of recipients is shown in Table 1.

Many people do not meet national insurance contribution conditions and severe disablement allowance provides for people who are incapable of work but do not satisfy the contribution requirements for incapacity benefit. Today, claimants must be aged between 16 and 65 when they make their claim, but there is no upper age limit for receiving the allowance once it has been awarded. Claimants must have been incapable of work for at least 28 weeks. The claimant receives £40.35 per week (1999/2000 rates) and adult dependants £23.95, plus extra for children. Age-related additions are payable. A person under 40, for example, receives an extra £14.05 a week. There were 363,940 recipients of SDA at the end of February 1997.[47]

Table 1

GB, thousands

	Number of Recipients at a date								
	1982	1987	1992	1993	1994	1995	1996	1997	1998
Sickness Benefit	393	110	138	147	127	127	-	-	-
Invalidity Benefit	683	968	1,439	1,580	1,681	1,767	-	-	-
Incapacity Benefit	-	-	-	-	-	-	1,813	1,749	1,645
Severe Disablement Allowance	143	260	302	316	329	348	344	364	371

Source: Social Security Statistics, 1997; DSS, IB and SDA Quarterly Summary of Statistics, May 1998.

The chief problem with incapacity benefits is that individuals are allowed to present partial information about themselves to the authorities. If they can 'pass' the 'all work' test by the use of 'tactics' or 'tips' the system is fair game. This attitude may be compared with that engendered by the friendly societies.

When national insurance was first enacted in Britain in 1911, over three-quarters of those covered by the scheme were already members of mutual aid associations, known as friendly societies. The paramount purpose of the friendly societies was independence. They provided all the services that enabled individuals to be self-supporting. If illness or injury struck, the friendly societies provided both a cash benefit and medical care, usually available through each society's own doctor, who was typically paid a capitation fee in return for free care.

The success of the friendly societies was the result of the face-to-face involvement of members in the local branches which administered benefits. The members knew who was paying. It was not an anonymous 'them' but the members themselves. Moreover, the societies did not merely pay benefits. They also arranged for sick members to be visited at least once a week, and in some cases every day. The regular visits provided companionship and practical help to members and helped to avoid fraud. There was no possibility of using tactics to pass a twenty-minute medical in the presence of a doctor meeting you for the first and last time.

There is a strong feeling among many officials in the DSS that a proportion of claimants are 'swinging the lead'. Their view was expressed by Frank Field shortly after his resignation in July 1998:

> Somebody who becomes unemployed, for example, soon realises that they are significantly worse off than if they could become classified as long-term sick...
> The result is no surprise. Large numbers of claimants graduate from unemployment to incapacity benefit. While for many this is the right and proper action, for others it is merely a means of getting more money.[48]

The work test is in urgent need of reform. At present the classification is very clear-cut: a person is capable of work or not. The Government has already announced that it intends to introduce a new medical examination intended to establish how much work can be performed.[49] The expectation will be that each person will do as much work as their limitations allow—the approach adopted in Wisconsin. Of course, some people will prove to be incapable of any work at all and it goes without saying that they should continue to receive benefit.

Such proposals would mean cancelling the main income replacement benefits in favour of transitional assistance. This would mean scrapping income-based JSA, contribution-based JSA, income support, incapacity benefit and severe disablement allowance so that there would be no sharp distinction between people who can work and people who cannot, nor any distinction between contributory and non-contributory benefits. Every person would be expected to contribute as much as his or her abilities allowed.

Low Wages

What should be done about people in work who are genuinely able to earn very little? The problem has been that measures so far taken to subsidise low incomes from work have led to reductions in work effort, either by couples or lone parents. As Chapter 1 showed, this has been one of the main defects of family credit. The least defensible aspect of both family credit and working families tax credit is that benefit is paid to people who work as few as 16 hours a week. In effect, by working only part time, individuals can have their wages made up to the equivalent of a full-time week's work.

The guiding principles of reform should be that individuals are responsible for improving their income and for controlling their expenses. If a person has made a reasonable effort to earn as much as possible and is still on an unacceptably low income, in-work benefits may be defensible. It is not possible for public officials to judge in detail whether a given individual or family has made a reasonable effort to increase earnings and control expenses, but it would be feasible to apply a simple administrative rule.

One such test of 'reasonable effort' could be based on the number of hours worked. The figure could be about 40 hours a week for one or two parents with children under school age, or 50 hours once the children are at school (thus releasing the second parent to work part time). If working families tax credit were abolished and replaced by such a system of 40/50-hour supplements, the benefit system would reward hard work, and be far more appealing to married couples with a hard-working single earner and far less appealing to single parents.

The Taxation of Families

The working families tax credit has one merit, namely that it tries to adopt an integrated approach to taxes and benefits. Many families with relatively low incomes are paying taxes as well as receiving in-work benefits. This became a major problem during the 1960s when Labour Governments dramatically increased the tax burden. This is shown by comparing the break-even point in the late 1940s with the figure today.

Each year the Inland Revenue publishes the break-even point for a married couple with two children under 11. The break-even point is the tax threshold plus the earnings point at which tax payable is equal to child benefit (or in earlier years, family allowance). For recipients of child benefit this point is their real tax threshold. This break-even point is expressed as a percentage of average earnings and calculations have been made back to 1949-50 (Figure 1, p. 105).

These figures show that many people have been taxed into low income. In 1952 the break-even point for a married man with two children under 11 was 104 per cent of average earnings. In 1975-76 it was 45 per cent, the lowest point. In 1997-98 it was 48 per cent. In cash terms, the break-even point was £10,306 per annum in 1997-98, or £198.19 per week. The most significant changes came in the late 1960s. In 1961-62, the figure was 83 per cent. By 1969-70 it had fallen to 62 per cent.

The position would be much improved by replacing child benefit with income tax allowances for children. Tax allowances permit people to keep their own money and thereby encourage a sense of personal responsibility. Benefits tend to have the opposite effect. The chief argument against tax allowances is that people who have no tax liability (because their income is below the tax threshold) do not benefit. The counter argument is that the existence of the allowance gives people an incentive to earn more so that they are able to take advantage of the whole tax allowance, still further encouraging self-sufficiency. For this reason, child benefit should be scrapped and replaced by child tax allowances.

To further reinforce marriage, married couples should each receive a personal tax allowance (as at present) but they should be free to transfer it to the other partner. They should also receive a transferrable married person's allowance (as at present) but it should be applied to the highest rate of tax paid (unlike at present). The ability to transfer allowances should be confined to married couples.

Provision For Possible Misfortunes

I turn now to the second obligation of the citizen: to provide against misfortunes, which might interrupt self-sufficiency. Ill health and disability are insurable, and provision could easily be private to allow room for commercial insurers and mutual aid associations to offer services. There is already a flourishing private sector offering sick pay—or permanent health insurance, as it is now called—and these organisations could easily expand their role.

Private insurance should not be compulsory. Insurance is not the only method of protection against contingencies and many people may prefer other methods of self-sufficiency, including simple saving, or investment in shares, or to purchase property or durable goods which can be sold if the need arises.

There have long been private insurance schemes to share risks with others, many of which were effectively nationalised by the 1911 national insurance scheme. The chief difficulty about insurance is that it is a mechanism designed for people who wish to guard against an event that has not already happened. If we decide to restore to civil society provision against the cost of income replacement during illness, insurance will not be available to people who are already ill or disabled. The Government should continue to provide for them and honour existing commitments.

Provision For The Lifecycle

The third obligation of the citizen is to take responsibility for 'income smoothing' over the lifecycle. For the great majority of people two stages of the lifecycle put the family budget under particular strain. First, raising children adds to costs at a time when income may fall if one partner concentrates on childcare. And second, as age takes its toll, income may fall due to retirement from work, and expenses may rise due to failing health or the need for social or nursing care.

Since 1925 British governments have used their powers of compulsion to require people to contribute towards a pension, and since 1948, when family allowance was introduced, the state has taken part of the responsibility for redirecting earnings towards families with children. In practice, it has assumed responsibility for the two main periods of the lifecycle when expenditure is in danger of exceeding available resources.

How can compulsion be defended? Provision for child raising was the subject of the previous section and I will concentrate now on provision for old age.

Pension provision illustrates the chief dilemmas. Is it realistic to expect people to take personal responsibility for self-support during old age? Of course, there should be an infallible safety net. But it is widely accepted that the presence of a safety net may encourage some individuals to rely on the state rather than their own endeavours. This difficulty is at the heart of the current debate about pension reform. To what extent should provision of a pension be compulsory? At present the basic pension is compulsory, and so too is payment towards the state earnings related pension (SERPS), although individuals can opt to pay their national insurance contributions into a personal pension.

Despite being contributory, both the basic pension and SERPS are pay-as-you-go systems, financed from current tax revenues and not from a separate fund. (The Government's green paper on pensions proposes only minor changes in this structure.)[50] Advocates of compulsory provision by the state usually recommend one of two main alternatives: either a funded state pension, such as Singapore's; or a compulsory funded private pension of which the Chilean scheme is the prime example.

The strongest argument for compulsion is that, if the state maintains a safety net, then some individuals will be more likely to rely on it rather than to provide for themselves. Therefore, so the argument goes, people who are capable of saving but do not or will not, should be required to do so. But, should the desire to avoid free riding outweigh all other considerations?

What are the potential disadvantages of compulsion?

1. A compulsory pension is defended as a means of eliminating free riders, but it does not completely achieve that objective. Some people never earn enough to accumulate a pension fund. Some refrain from work. Some work in the black economy. Moreover, compulsion increases the incentives to work 'off the books'. Countries with compulsory schemes, such as Chile, still have to maintain a state guarantee funded from taxes.

2. Compulsion is applied to people who would have saved anyway. Many are compelled to save in a manner which may not be the best for them. A self-employed person, for example, may prefer to invest in his own business and such an investment may well prove to be a more sound method of provision than a compulsory contribution to an annuity.

3. Compelling individuals to contribute a fixed percentage of their income to a private pension throughout life assumes a stable pattern of employment. But the pattern of work has changed. Earlier in the century it was possible to assume that most people were employees, but this is no longer true. The labour market continues to change, with far fewer workers now

expecting to spend their career with one employer and many more preferring self-employment. A compulsory scheme crowds out flexible alternatives that would allow adjustment to changing circumstances.

4. A compulsory scheme, based on a percentage of income, also fails to acknowledge the legitimacy of changes in saving and spending priorities over the lifecycle. The importance of the risks we face changes over time. It is legitimate to have different priorities when younger. For example, when a married couple have children to support then the death of the breadwinner would be very serious, as would incapacity for work. But when the children are grown up, early death is less important.

5. Inevitably a compulsory scheme must be regulated, and the regulations limit the access of new companies to the market and diminish the scope for innovative competition. In Chile, for example, a relatively small number of regulated companies have a guaranteed market. The result is that they do not need to try so hard.

6. To contribute to a pension by locking away savings for 20–30 years is not the most prudent savings strategy. To hand over money today to a private company knowing that you will be forced to buy an annuity in 2028 is inherently risky. The company might be a mutual at the moment, but what will it be in the future? Companies can and do increase their charges (which might be from 13 per cent to 39 per cent of contributions); investment performance varies; annuity rates fluctuate; policy towards bonuses may change; and the government might change the tax regime again. These uncertainties explain why in 1998, after only a few years, about 6.5 million people had invested £105 billion in PEPs and TESSAs, despite their less favourable tax treatment. They are popular because they allow people to move their savings in the light of changing circumstances. It is not short-sighted to want to avoid relinquishing control of your retirement income. It is prudent.

7. The idea of a pension assumes retirement from work, but not everyone wishes to 'retire', preferring to lead a 'useful life' until they die or become incapable of work. Most people retiring at 65 are capable of working for many more years.

8. If the government sets a percentage of income that must be paid anticipating that it will produce a fund at retirement sufficient to yield an annuity of a certain amount, what happens when investment performance is poor or annuity rates are bad? In practice, the government may find that it comes under pressure to guarantee investment performance.

Thus, compulsion does not achieve its primary objective—to avoid free riding—but it has a harmful effect on other people, many of whom would have made sensible provision. These are arguments against compulsion but they are also strong arguments against tax concessions. If compulsion is a *requirement* to put money into a bad investment, tax breaks are an *inducement* to put money into a bad bet. The objective of policy should, therefore, be to create a regulatory framework which allows the maximum flexibility whilst guarding against fraud and financial abuse. Before suggesting how such a framework could be established, it will be useful to examine more fully whether it is feasible to rely on personal responsibility. The assumptions still being made by many politicians belong in the age of social determinism, whereas we are now in a new era of personal responsibility—or, for post-modernists who prefer to clothe long-established ideas in new language, an age of personal 'risk management'.

Alternative Lifecycle Strategies

Are there other strategies that a prudent and unselfish person could pursue? And if so, why should the Government make it more difficult for them? I will suggest two such strategies.

First, there is 'work till you drop'. A prudent person could plan to go on working until he was no longer able to do so. In some cases such a person would die while still working, and in others he would work until illness or frailty intervened. The main risk is that a relatively young person may become too ill or frail to work, and so a prudent person would ensure that he had a disability insurance policy, payable at any age, and which preferably paid a high income replacement benefit linked to salary. But, as we have seen, if an individual were compelled to pay a percentage of his income into a pension, his ability to provide for possible misfortunes would be diminished. A person pursuing a 'work till you drop' strategy would be self-sufficient and at no stage of his life a burden on other people.

The former is a one-generation strategy, but it would be perfectly prudent for a family to follow a two- or three-generation plan. A family could build up assets—property, durable goods, shares, cash—with the intention of handing them on from generation to generation. Purchasing an annuity involves giving a capital sum to an insurance company which undertakes to pay an agreed sum per year until death. The insurer takes the risk that the capital will run out, but members of a family might prefer to take that risk them-selves. If the oldest surviving generation, for example, opts to live on its capital rather than to buy an annuity, the risk of their capital running out before they die gives their children an incentive to diminish expenditure, perhaps by caring for their parents them-selves. They might use the capital to build a 'granny annex', so that their parents were close at hand. Or they might purchase 'long term care insurance' to guard against the high cost of residential care.

Such a property-based strategy offers considerable flexibility for families of quite modest means. For most people, investing in the family home has been a good bet for much of this century and by trading up or down, or using the property as collateral for a loan, cash can be made available at different stages of the lifecycle. It has also been the strategy successfully pursued by some of the poorest overseas immigrants to this country.

Of course, parents could find not only that their capital had run out, but also that their children proved unreliable. However, the danger of falling back on the state safety net could be avoided by simultaneously pursuing the 'work till you drop' strategy. Encour-agement of a cross-generational approach would, incidentally, have the added advantage of being a considerably more effective method of strengthening families than widening the powers of health visitors and marriage registrars, as proposed in the Government's green paper on families.[51]

A New Policy Framework for Old Age

Thus, there are alternative strategies which could be pursued without free riding, but is it possible for the government to create a new framework which maintains a safety net, minimises free riding, and encourages personal responsibility?

The temptation to free ride is the result of offering unconditional benefit payments on reaching a certain age. The Government has accepted that this system creates a moral hazard, but it has chosen to deal with it by coercing people who do not need to be coerced, many of whom have made arrangements more suitable for their own circumstances than any pension, whether a basic state pension, the State Earnings Related Pension, or the proposed State Second Pension.[52] Moreover, by proposing to pay the State Second Pension at a flat rate, regardless of contributions, the Government has increased the temptation to free ride.

A more effective method of removing the moral hazard would be to abolish the state retirement age. Thus, individuals of any age who relied on state benefits would be obliged to find a job or take part in a government work scheme. If a work obligation is attached to benefits at all ages, there is little temptation to take advantage. The obligation to work, obviously, should only apply to people who are capable of it and individuals who are too ill, injured or frail should be able to fall back on the safety net.

If the safety net were a system of transitional relief, as I have argued, this would mean that elderly persons claiming benefit would have to undergo a medical examination to show that they were unable to be fully self-sufficient. It can be argued that tests of fitness for work should not be necessary after a certain age. Perhaps so, but age 65 is too young. We now live much longer and enjoy good health well beyond 65 and an alternative approach would be to raise the pension age in stages, perhaps by six months per year so that in ten years it will be 70 and in 20 years, 75. Having achieved the relevant age, no test of fitness for work would be necessary and the basic state pension would be payable.

Eventually, the pension age could be phased out altogether so that we would no longer become members of the demeaning category 'old-age pensioner' towards the end of our lives. Instead of having a group identity imposed on us by the system, we would continue to play our part as individuals, each with a unique contribution to make.

Finally, the current tax regime for pensions should be revised. If compelling people to contribute to a pension is wrong, so too is offering them a tax inducement. A better system would be to replace it with the tax regime for PEPs and now ISAs, but with much higher investment limits. Schemes could then evolve with the minimum of regulation offering any combination of saving, protective insurance, investment for income or capital growth, long-term lock-in, short-term access, linkage or non-linkage to annuities.

The regulatory framework would be lighter, a trend already under way now that benchmarks have been preferred over top-heavy regulation for ISAs. The ISA CAT mark is an example of what could be achieved in the rest of the financial services sector. Vast opportunities would be opened up for innovative and enterprising companies. And it would maximise self-sufficiency and independence for the people whilst ensuring that no one could fall below a clear national minimum income.

Conclusions

In recent years the trend has been to understand poverty as a misfortune that just happens through 'no fault of our own'. But when we say a person is poor, what do we mean? As Chapter 1 showed, Seebohm Rowntree, who dominated poverty analysis during the first half of the century, explained poverty as the result of changes in relative income and expenditure over the lifecycle. During a typical person's adult life, he would be likely to encounter two stages when expenditure would be high compared with his income. The first results from increased expenditure due to the cost of raising children and the second from a fall in income due to complete or partial retirement from paid work.

However, in neither case is the individual completely powerless to influence events. A couple can control their expenses during child raising by limiting their family and reducing other outgoings such as housing costs and luxuries. Moreover, they can save in preparation for the expense of raising children both while they are single and when married but before children come along.

Similarly an imbalance between income and expenditure in old age can be avoided either by saving in earlier years, continuing to work (when possible), or by reducing expenses.

Our personal decisions make a big difference to the extent of any imbalance between expenditure and income. However, from this statement it does not follow that every person who struggles to make ends meet is to 'blame', nor even that their predicament is entirely their own fault. But they may be responsible to some extent and if so we should say so, because any lasting remedy will involve behavioural change on their part.

Those who treat poverty as always and everywhere the result of sheer misfortune eliminate from consideration measures that, in practice, are most likely to help. It goes without saying that the truly powerless victim of outside events should always be helped. Indeed, the person who has brought problems on himself should also always be helped. The choice is not between help and neglect, but between methods of help that entrench the problem and methods that bring a lasting solution.

It is sometimes said that the welfare state has encouraged altruism, and it is further claimed that to base welfare on self-help will encourage selfishness. In truth, the one-sided welfare rights culture has encouraged a selfish attitude to claiming benefits at the general expense. And encouraging more self-sufficiency will not bring about more selfishness, but restore to individuals the capacity to make a positive contribution to the well-being of others.

A sense of community is built on the self-sufficiency of individuals and families. The alternative to self-sufficiency is to rely on other people, and so it is an extraordinary abuse of language to associate self-sufficiency with selfishness. Self-help is neither a synonym, nor a euphemism, for selfishness, but means equipping ourselves to help others.

Figure 1

Tax Break-Even Point, 1949-1998

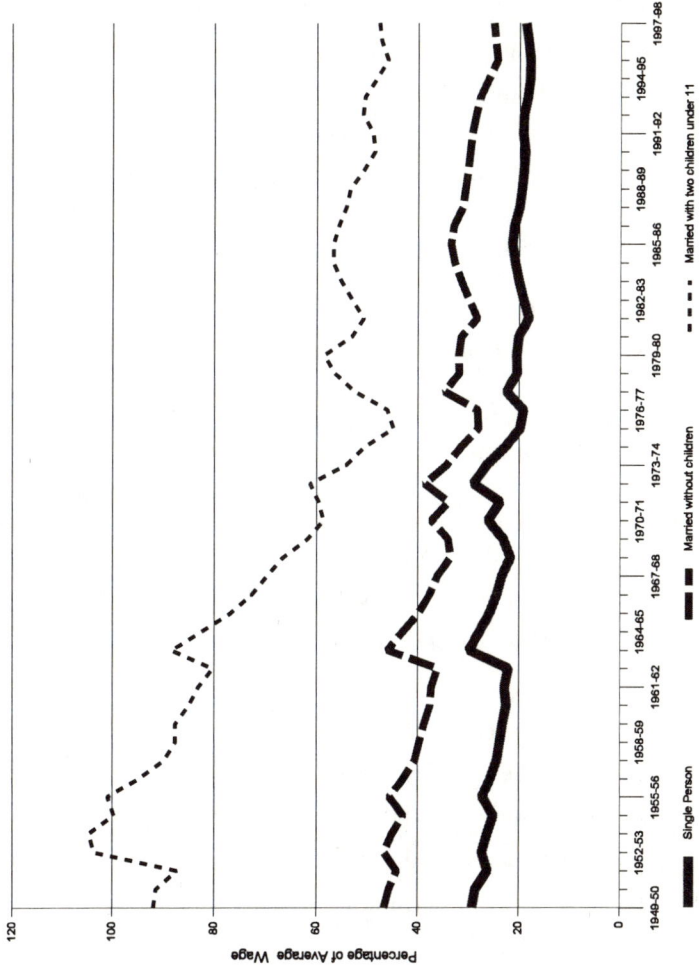

106

Notes

Chapter 1: New Labour's Strategy for the Workless

1 *New Ambitions for Our Country: A New Contract for Welfare*, Cm 3805, London: Stationery Office, March 1998, p. 25.

2 DSS/DfEE, *A New Contract For Welfare: The Gateway to Work*, Cm 4102, October 1998, p. 2.

3 *New Ambitions for Our Country*, Cm 3805,1998, p. 1.

4 *New Ambitions for Britain*, Financial Statement and Budget Report, March 1998, House of Commons No. 620, p. 51.

5 The Working Families Tax Credit, *The Modernisation of Britain's Tax and Benefit System,* Number 3. London: HM Treasury, 1998, para. 1.04.

6 *New Ambitions for Our Country*, Cm 3805,1998, p. 44.

7 A useful summary can be found in Marsh, A., 'Lowering barriers to work in Britain', *Social Policy Journal of New Zealand*, Issue 8, March 1997, pp. 111-135.

8 Ford, R., 'The role of childcare in lone mothers' decisions whether or not to work', in DSS, *Research Yearbook 1996/97*, London: HMSO, 1997, p. 67.

9 Ford, 'The role of childcare...', 1997, p. 67.

10 Ford, 'The role of childcare...', p. 67.

11 Ford, 'The role of childcare...', p. 68.

12 Ford, 'The role of childcare...', p. 68.

13 Ford, 'The role of childcare...', p. 72.

14 Ford, 'The role of childcare...', p. 69.

15 Ford, 'The role of childcare...', p. 69.

16 Ford, 'The role of childcare...', p. 64.

17 Ford, 'The role of childcare...', p. 63.

18 Ford, 'The role of childcare...', p. 63.

19 Marsh, *SPJNZ*, 1997, p. 129.

20 Mead, L., *The New Politics of Poverty*, New York: Basic Books, 1992, p. 171.

21 McKay, S. and Marsh, A., *Why Didn't They Claim?*, London: PSI, 1995, p. 14.

22 McKay and Marsh, *Why Didn't They Claim?*, p. 42.

23 McKay and Marsh, *Why Didn't They Claim?*, p. 25.

24 Marsh, A. and McKay, S., *Families, Work and Benefits*, London: PSI, 1993, p. 185.

25 Marsh, *SPJNZ*, 1997, p. 118.

26 Marsh, *SPJNZ*, p. 132.

27 Marsh, A., 'How family credit works', *Social Security Research Yearbook 1994/95, London: HMSO,* 1995, pp. 26-27.

28 Marsh, *SPJNZ*, 1997, p. 125.

29 Marsh, *SPJNZ*, p. 112.

30 Marsh, *SPJNZ*, p. 119.

31 Marsh, *SPJNZ*, p. 120.

32 Shaw, A., Walker, R., Ashworth, K., Jenkins, S. and Middleton, S., *Moving Off Income Support: Barriers and Bridges*, DSS Research Report No. 53, London: HMSO, 1996, p. 114.

33 DSS, *Family Credit Statistics, Quarterly Enquiry*, February 1998.

34 Marsh and McKay, *Families, Work and Benefits*, 1993, p. 9.

35 Marsh and McKay, *Families, Work and Benefits*, p. 27.

36 Marsh and McKay, *Families, Work and Benefits*, p. 102.

37 Bryson, A., Ford, R., and White, M., *Making Work Pay: Lone Mothers, Employment and Well-Being*, York: Joseph Rowntree Foundation, 1997, p. 39.

38 Millar, J., Webb, S. and Kemp, M., *Combining Work and Welfare*, York: Joseph Rowntree Foundation, 1997, p. 31.

39 Marsh and McKay, *Families, Work and Benefits*, 1993, p. 186.

40 Marsh, *SPJNZ*, 1997, p. 126.

41 DSS, *Family Credit Statistics, Quarterly Enquiry*, February 1998, p. 17.

42 Marsh, *Social Security Research Yearbook 1994/95*, 1995, p. 25.

43 Marsh, *SPJNZ*, 1997, p. 124.

44 Millar, J., Webb, S. and Kemp, M., *Combining Work and Welfare*, York: Joseph Rowntree Foundation, 1997, p. 26.

45 *New Ambitions For Our Country*, Cm 3805, 1998, p. 2. See also Mr Blair's Foreword, p. v.

46 *The Times*, 15 January 1998.

47 *New Ambitions For Our Country*, Cm 3805, 1998, p. iii.

48 For an excellent discussion of the legacy of Titmuss, see Deacon, A., 'Richard Titmuss: 20 years on', *Journal of Social Policy*, vol. 22, part 2, April 1993, pp. 235-42. Elsewhere Professor Deacon has described the influence as a kind of intellectual 'treacle' clogging rational debate.

49 Phillips, M., 'The Sex-Change State', SMF Memorandum, London: Social Market Foundation, 1998.

50 Hansard, 19 March 1998.

51 Giddens, A., *The Third Way*, Cambridge: Polity Press, 1998, p. 92.

52 Giddens, *The Third Way*, p. 93.

53 Giddens, *The Third Way*, p. 93.

54 Giddens, *The Third Way*, p. 94.

55 Giddens, *The Third Way*, p. 94.

56 Giddens, *The Third Way*, p. 92.

57 McLanahan, S. and Sandefur, G., *Growing Up with a Single Parent: What Hurts, What Helps*, Cambridge, MA and London: Harvard University Press, 1994.

58 Giddens, *The Third Way*, p. 97.

59 *Financial Times*, 31 March 1998.

60 DSS, Tax/Benefit Model Tables, April 1997, p. 1.6.7.

61 The Working Families Tax Credit and Work Incentives, Modernisation No. 3, HM Treasury, 1998, p. 16.

Chapter 2: Changing Attitudes to Poverty and Independence

1 This account is based on the description given in the Poor Law Report of 1834, pp. 4-7.

2 Poor Law Report of 1834, p. 5.

3 Poor Law Report of 1834, p. 6.

4 Tocqueville, A. de, *Memoir on Pauperism*, London: IEA, 1997.

5 Macfarlane, A., *The Origins of English Individualism*, Oxford: Blackwell, 1978.

6 Poor Law Report of 1834, p. 12.

7 Poor Law Report of 1834, p. 12.

8 Poor Law Report of 1834, p. 16.

9 Poor Law Report of 1834, pp. 16-17.

10 Poor Law Report of 1834, pp. 18-19.

11 Poor Law Report of 1834, p. 21.

12 Poor Law Report of 1834, p. 24.

13 Poor Law Report of 1834, p. 127.

14 Poor Law Report of 1834, p. 127.

15 Poor Law Report of 1834, p. 146.

16 Poor Law Report of 1834, pp. 32-33.

17 Poor Law Report of 1834, p. 25.

18 Himmelfarb, G., *The Idea of Poverty*, London: Faber, 1984, p. 162; Poor Law Report of 1834, pp. 28-29.

19 Poor Law Report of 1834, pp. 28-29.

20 Poor Law Report of 1834, p. 44.

21 Poor Law Report of 1834, p. 49.

22 Poor Law Report of 1834, p. 147.

23 Poor Law Report of 1834, p. 123.

24 Himmelfarb, *The Idea of Poverty*, 1984, p. 165; Poor Law Report of 1834, p. 148.

25 For example, Fraser, D., *The Evolution of the British Welfare State*, London: Macmillan, 1978, pp. 40, 44-45.

26 Poor Law Report of 1834, p. 100.

27 Poor Law Report of 1834, p. 128.

28 Poor Law Report of 1834, pp. 128-9.

29 Poor Law Report of 1834, p. 129.

30 Poor Law Report of 1834, p. 129.

31 Poor Law Report of 1834, p. 130.

32 Poor Law Report of 1834, p. 130.

33 Poor Law Report of 1834, p. 131.

34 Poor Law Report of 1834, p. 131.

35 Poor Law Report of 1834, p. 131.

36 Poor Law Report of 1834, p. 146.

37 Poor Law Report of 1834, p. 133.

38 Poor Law Report of 1834, p. 134.

39 Poor Law Report of 1834, p. 135.

40 Poor Law Report of 1834, p. 148.

41 Poor Law Report of 1834, p. 141.

42 Quoted in Gosden, P.H.J.H., *Self Help*, London: Batsford, 1973, p. 64. (Emphasis added.)

43 Bosanquet, H., *The Poor Law Report of 1909*, London: Macmillan, 1909.

44 Bosanquet, *The Poor Law Report of 1909,* p. 3.

45 Bosanquet, H., *The Strength of the People*, London, Macmillan, 1903, second edition, p. 110.

46 Bosanquet, *The Strength of the People*, p. 110.

47 Bosanquet, *The Poor Law Report of 1909,* p. 4.

48 Bosanquet, *The Poor Law Report of 1909*, p. 5.

49 Bosanquet, *The Poor Law Report of 1909*, p. 6.

50 Bosanquet, *The Poor Law Report of 1909*, pp. 7-8.

51 Bosanquet, *The Poor Law Report of 1909*, pp. 8-9.

52 Bosanquet, *The Poor Law Report of 1909*, p. 109.

53 Bosanquet, *The Poor Law Report of 1909*, p. 109.

54 Bosanquet, *The Poor Law Report of 1909*, p. 39.

55 Bosanquet, *The Poor Law Report of 1909*, p. 39.

56 Bosanquet, *The Strength of the People*, 1903, p. 108.

57 Booth, C. *Life and Labour of the People in London*, London: Macmillan, 1902. (4 vols.) vol. 2, p. 21.

58 Booth, 1902, vol. 1, p. 131.

59 Booth, vol. 1, p. 167.

60 Booth, vol. 1, p. 168.

61 Booth, vol. 1, p. 169.

62 Booth, vol. 1, p. 131.

63 Rowntree, B.S., *Poverty: A Study of Town Life*, 2nd edition, London: Nelson, 1901, pp. 117-18.

64 Beveridge, W.H., *Social Insurance and Allied Services*, Cmnd 6404, London: HMSO, 1942, pp. 211-12.

65 Supplementary Benefits Commission, Annual Report,1976, p. 204.

66 Beveridge, *Social Insurance and Allied Services*, Cmnd 6404, 1942, pp. 212-213.

67 Rowntree, B.S., *Poverty and Progress*, London: Longmans, 1941, p. vi.

68 Rowntree, *Poverty and Progress*, p. 108.

69 Rowntree, *Poverty: A Study of Town Life*, 1901, pp. 170-71.

70 Rowntree, *Poverty: A Study of Town Life*, p. 171.

71 Rowntree, *Poverty: A Study of Town Life*, p. 173.

72 Rowntree, *Poverty and Progress*, 1941, p. 161.

73 Rowntree, *Poverty and Progress*, pp. 164-71.

74 Beveridge, *Social Insurance and Allied Services*, Cmnd 6404, 1942, para. 11. See Harris, J., *William Beveridge: A Biography*, 2nd edition, Oxford: Clarendon Press, 1997, pp. 381-82.

75 *Beveridge, Social Insurance and Allied Services*, Cmnd 6404, para. 13.

76 *Beveridge, Social Insurance and Allied Services*, Cmnd 6404, para. 15.

77 Harris, J., *William Beveridge*, 1997, p. 383, 410.

78 Rowntree, *Poverty and Progress*, 1941, p. 477.

Chapter 3: The Rise and Decline of Egocentric Collectivism

1 Harrington, M., *The Other America: Poverty in the United States*, Baltimore: Penguin, 1963.

2 Harrington, *The Other America*, p. 171.

3 Harrington, *The Other America*, pp. 173-74.

4 Harrington, *The Other America*, p. 174.

5 Harrington, *The Other America*, p. 175.

6 Abel-Smith, B., and Townsend, P., *The Poor and the Poorest*, London: Bell, 1965, pp. 21-22.

7 Abel-Smith and Townsend, *The Poor and the Poorest*, pp. 39-40, 65.

8 Dennis, N., *Rising Crime and the Dismembered Family*, London: IEA , 1993; and *The Invention of Permanent Poverty*, London: IEA, 1997.

9 Magnet, M. *The Dream and the Nightmare*, New York: William Morrow, 1993. For a discussion of the issues see my earlier book, *From Welfare State to Civil Society*, Wellington: NZBR, 1996.

10 Hayek, F.A., *The Constitution of Liberty*, London: Routledge, 1960, esp. Chapter 6; Hayek, F.A., *Law, Legislation and Liberty: the Mirage of Social Justice* (vol. 2 of 3 vols.), London: Routledge, 1976.

11 Mead, L., *Beyond Entitlement: The Social Obligations of Citizenship*, New York: The Free Press, 1986, p. 57.

12 Novak, M. *et al.*, *The New Consensus on Family and Welfare*, Washington: American Enterprise Institute, 1987.

13 Fukuyama, F., *The End of History and the Last Man*, London: Penguin, 1992.

14 Fukuyama, F., *Trust: The Social Virtues and the Creation of Prosperity*, London: Hamish Hamilton, 1995, pp. 4-5.

15 Fukuyama, *Trust*, p. 11.

16 Coleman, J., *Foundations of Social Theory*, London: Harvard University Press, 1994, pp. 300-21.

17 Sowell, T., *Conquests and Cultures*, New York: Basic Books, 1998, p. 339.

18 McLanahan, S. and Sandefur, G., *Growing Up with a Single Parent: What Hurts, What Helps*, Cambridge, MA: Harvard University Press, 1994, pp. 1-2.

19 MacIntyre, A., *After Virtue*, London: Duckworth, 1985.

20 Green, D.G., *Community Without Politics: A Market Approach to Welfare Reform*, London: IEA, 1995; Olasky, M., *The Tragedy of American Compassion*, Washington: Regnery Gateway, 1992; Tanner, M., *The End of Welfare: Fighting Poverty in Civil Society*, Washington: Cato Institute, 1996.

21 *Making Work Pay: Taxation, Benefits, Employment and Unemployment*, Paris: OECD, 1997. James Cox provides an excellent description of the limitations of this approach in Cox, J., *Towards Personal Independence and Prosperity*, Wellington: NZBR, 1997.

22 Mead, L.M. (ed.), *The New Paternalism: Supervisory Approaches to Poverty*, Washington: Brookings, 1997.

23 Ellwood, D., *Poor Support*, New York: Basic Books, 1988, pp. ix-x.

24 Ellwood, *Poor Support*, p. x.

25 Ellwood, *Poor Support*, p. 19.

26 Ellwood, *Poor Support*, p. 21.

27 Ellwood, *Poor Support*, p. 25.

28 Ellwood, *Poor Support*, p. 43.

29 Ellwood, *Poor Support*, p. 44.

30 Ellwood, *Poor Support*, p. 156.

31 Ellwood, *Poor Support*, p. 9.

32 Ellwood, *Poor Support*, p. 184.

33 Ellwood, *Poor Support*, pp. 87, 89.

Chapter 4: Poverty, Work and Public Policy

1 Rogers, J., 'Designing work-focused welfare replacement programmes', *Social Policy Journal of New Zealand*, Issue 8, March 1997, p. 68.

2 Rogers, *SPJNZ*, p. 73.

3 Rogers, *SPJNZ*, p. 75.

4   Rogers, *SPJNZ*, pp. 71,76; Mead, L., *From Welfare to Work: Lessons From America*, London: IEA, 1997; Mead, L. (ed.), *The New Paternalism: Supervisory Approaches to Poverty*, Washington, DC: Brookings Institution, 1997.

5   For example Field, F., *Stakeholder Welfare*, London: IEA, 1996.

6   Mead, *From Welfare to Work*, 1997.

7   George, V., *Social Security: Beveridge and After*, London: Routledge, 1968, p. 233.

8   Supplementary Benefits Commission, Annual Report 1975, paras 3.1 and 3.2.

9   Supplementary Benefits Commission, Annual Report 1975, para 3.3.

10 George, *Social Security,* 1968, p. 232.

11 Supplementary Benefits Commission, Annual Report 1975, Cmnd 6615, p. 74.

12 Supplementary Benefits Commission, Annual Report, 1979, p. 173.

13 Supplementary Benefits Commission, Annual Report, 1979, p. 91.

14 Supplementary Benefits Commission, Annual Report, 1978, p. 14.

15 Supplementary Benefits Commission, Annual Report, 1978, p. 116.

16 Social Services Committee, Second Report, Session 1985-86, *Resettlement Units and Re-establishment Centres*, Appendix 2 and Appendix 3.

17 George, *Social Security,* 1968, p. 232.

18 DHSS, Annual Report 1972, Cmnd 5352, p. 113.

19 Supplementary Benefits Commission, Annual Report, 1978, p. 116.

20 Supplementary Benefits Commission, Annual Report, 1979, Appendix A, p. 211.

21 The Report of the Committee on Abuse of Social Security Benefits, March 1973, Cmnd 5228, p. 106.

22 Supplementary Benefits Commission, Annual Report, 1979, pp. 211-12.

23 Bryson, A. and Jacobs, J., *Policing the Workshy*, Aldershot: Avebury, 1992, p. 40.

24 The results for the US are summarised in McLanahan, S. and Sandefur, G., *Growing Up With a Single Parent: What Hurts, What Helps*, Cambridge, Mass: Harvard University Press, 1994.

25 Supplementary Benefits Commission, Annual Report, 1979, p. 8.

26 *Reform of Social Security: Programme for Change*, vol. 2, Cmnd 9518, June 1985, p. 24.

27 Supplementary Benefits Commission, Annual Report, 1976, p. 121.

28 *New Statesman*, 3 December 1971.

29 Supplementary Benefits Commission, Annual Report, 1979, p. 151.

30 Reform of Social Security Background Papers, vol. 3. Cmnd 9519, p. 68.

31 From Green, D.G., *Benefit Dependency*, London: IEA, 1998.

32 Rowlingson, K., *et al*, *Social Security Fraud: the Role of Penalties*, DSS Research Report 64, London: HMSO, 1997, p. 24.

33 Marsh, A., 'Lowering the barriers to work in Britain', *Social Policy Journal of New Zealand*, Issue 8, March 1997, p. 131.

34 Marsh, *SPJNZ*, p. 131.

35 Quoted in George, *Social Security*, 1968, pp. 230-31.

36 DHSS, *Social Security Statistics 1982*, p. 219.

37 *Social Security Statistics 1992*, p. 39.

38 *Children First: A New Approach to Child Support*, July 1998, Cm 3992, p. 3.

39 For an excellent discussion of marriage as a contract see Barry, N. in Whelan, R. (ed.), *Just A Piece of Paper? Divorce Reform and the Undermining of Marriage*, London: IEA, 1995.

40 For an excellent discussion of the system in Switzerland and some Scandinavian countries see Segalman, R. and Marsland, D., *Cradle to Grave*, London: Macmillan, 1989.

41 Morgan, P., *Who Needs Parents?: The Effects of Childcare and Early Education on Children in Britain and the USA,* London: IEA, 1996.

42 McLanahan and Sandefur, *Growing Up With a Single Parent,* 1994.

43 Rogers, *SPJNZ,* 1997, p. 73.

44 CPAG's *Rights Guide to Non-Means-Tested Benefits*, p. 21.

45 CPAG's *Rights Guide to Non-Means-Tested Benefits*, p. 23.

46 DSS, IB and SDA Quarterly Summary of Statistics, 1997.

47 DSS, IB and SDA Quarterly Summary of Statistics, 1997.

48 *Sunday Times,* 2 August 1998.

49 DSS, *A New Contract For Welfare: Support for Disabled People*, Cm 4103, October 1998.

50 *A New Contract for Welfare: Partnership in Pensions*, Cm 4179, December 1998, London: Stationery Office.

51 *Supporting Families*: A Consultation Document, Stationery Office, November 1998.

52 *A New Contract for Welfare*, Cm 4179, December 1998.

117

Index

IEA Health and Welfare Unit

Advisory Council

Independence

The Health and Welfare Unit is part of the Institute of Economic Affairs, a registered educational charity (No. 235351) founded in 1955. Like the IEA, the Health and Welfare Unit is financed from a variety of private sources to avoid over-reliance on any single or small group of donors.

All IEA publications are independently refereed and referees' comments are passed on anonymously to authors. The IEA gratefully acknowledges the contributions made to its educational work by the eminent scholars who act as referees.

All the Institute's publications seek to further its objective of promoting the advancement of learning, by research into economic and political science, by education of the public therein, and by the dissemination of ideas, research and the results of research in these subjects. The views expressed are those of the authors, not of the IEA, which has no corporate view.